THE ONLY MIDDLE SCHOOL SURVIVAL GUIDE YOU'LL EVER NEED

TOOLS TO SQUASH ACADEMIC FEARS, CONQUER SOCIAL MEDIA PRESSURES WITH EASE & CONTROL YOUR EMOTIONS FOR CONFIDENCE & SUCCESS

DEBBIEANN LEWIS

CONTENTS

INTRODUCTION

Have you ever felt like middle school is just too much? Too much homework, too many social puzzles, too many changes all at once? Let me tell you about Jamie. Jamie was in the seventh grade when she faced one of her most brutal weeks: a science project due, a history essay, basketball tryouts, and, to top it all off, a falling out with her best friend. It felt like a mountain too high to climb. But here's the twist: it was also the week Jamie discovered her knack for organization and her passion for history. What seemed like her worst week turned out to be filled with hidden opportunities.

This is why I wrote this book. As someone who has spent years observing and interacting with middle school students, I've seen firsthand the struggles and triumphs of this pivotal time. From my days as a youth counselor to my professional journey in education, I've gathered stories and insights that can make your middle school years not just bearable but amazing!

This book is your ultimate middle school survival guide. It's crafted to help you navigate not just academics but also friendships, your evolving identity, and even your digital life. And yes, we'll tackle those overwhelming feelings, too. This isn't just another set of rules to follow; it's a map for finding your own path to joy, purpose, and success during these rollercoaster years.

We're going to take a unique approach here. Alongside practical advice and true stories, we'll look at why things work the way they do, both in your brain and in your social life. And don't worry – we'll keep things light with a dose of humor. Middle school might be tough, but who says we can't smile along the way?

You may be wondering how to use this guide; it's not a storybook you'll read from cover to cover; it's a guide! So, look up the subject, the question, or the topic in the table of contents and glean the advice for your middle school survival. For this guide to be helpful to you, check in with it, use it, and come back to it- it's all here in black and white for you to succeed. Remember, all the topics are laid out in easy steps to follow for excellent new skills to hone and for your survival today in middle school and confident success in your future.

So, this book is for you, the middle schooler who might be feeling a little lost or anxious about the road ahead. And to the educators and parents who are guiding these young adventurers: there are insights here for you, too. Together, let's uncover the strategies and secrets that can turn these years into a time of growth and discovery.

Get ready to dive into topics ranging from dealing with peer pressure to harnessing your personal strengths to juggling the demands of school life. We'll explore all this and more, with each chapter designed to empower and equip you for the journey.

So, turn the page. Let's start this adventure together, equipped with humor, science, and attitude. Middle school might be challenging, but remember: it's also full of opportunities to learn, grow, and thrive. Here's to discovering just how amazing your middle school years can be!

NAVIGATING SOCIAL SEAS

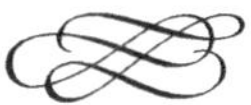

Let's dive straight into the wild waters of middle school friendships. Think of this chapter as your personal lifeboat in the sometimes stormy sea of social interactions. You know how it is—you're not a little kid anymore, but you're not quite a high schooler either. You're right in the thick of middle school, where every day can feel like a new episode of your favorite reality show, minus the fancy cameras and dramatic music. Here, friendships aren't just about who shares their candy with you or who likes the same video games. It's about finding your squad, the people who will stick by you when your science project flops or you accidentally trip in the hallway in front of everyone.

Navigating these waters can be tricky, so we will tackle the big friendship questions. How do you spot a true friend? What do you do when friendships start to wobble? And how on earth do you handle all the drama without losing your mind? Buckle up because we're about to get into the nitty-gritty of choosing your squad, understanding friendship dynamics, and keeping your ship afloat even when the waters get choppy.

1.1 CHOOSING YOUR SQUAD: HOW TO IDENTIFY GENUINE FRIENDSHIPS

So, how do you pick out the real-deal friends from the crowd? Imagine you're at lunch, sitting at that long table with your current crew. There's laughter, shared snacks, and a bunch of inside jokes. But how do you know who among them is genuine? Well, it starts with recognizing authenticity. Authentic friends are like gold in the murky river of middle school social life—they shine through because of their honesty, kindness, and empathy. Picture this: you flub your lines in the school play. A genuine friend doesn't laugh or let you stew in embarrassment; they're backstage, offering a high five and reminding you of all the lines you nailed.

Now, spotting these traits might sound like you need superpowers, but all it takes is a bit of observation. Watch how your friends treat others when they think no one is looking or how they talk about people who aren't there. Do they show kindness? Are they honest, even when it's tough? These clues can show you who's likely to be trustworthy and supportive in the long run.

Next up, think about what lights your fire. Are you into robotics, fantasy novels, or skateboarding? Shared interests can lay a rock-solid foundation for friendships. Dive into clubs, teams, or groups that align with what you love doing. It's there that you'll likely meet peers who are on the same wavelength. This isn't just about having fun together—it's about understanding and sharing passions that can deepen bonds.

But here's the kicker: even if someone shares your love for comic books or soccer, it's crucial to see how they fit into the bigger picture of your life. How do they handle stress or disagreements? Do they give as much as they take? Being in a friendship isn't so different from being on a team—you both need to pass the ball, share the victories, and sometimes, help each other up when one of you takes a tumble.

And speaking of tumbles, misunderstandings, and conflicts are part of any friendship. Maybe your friend forgot to save you a seat at lunch, or you both want to lead the group project. Instead of letting these moments push you apart, they can actually be stepping stones to stronger friendships. The key? Communication. Approach your friend calmly, explain how you feel, and listen to their side of the story. Often, just talking openly can patch up misunderstandings before they grow into bigger issues.

Interactive Element: Friendship Scenarios Quiz

To wrap up this part, why not put your new knowledge to the test? Take this quick quiz to see how you'd handle different friendship scenarios. Would you recognize a genuine friend? How would you deal with a misunderstanding? Your answers might surprise you!

<u>Friendship Scenarios Quiz</u>

1. Your friend forgot their lunch at home. What do you do?

    a) Share your lunch with them.
    b) Ignore it and eat your own lunch.
    c) Tease them about forgetting.

2. A new student joins your class and looks nervous. How do you react?

    a) Introduce yourself and ask if they want to play.
    b) Wait for someone else to talk to them.
    c) Ignore them and keep playing with your friends.

3. Your friend is feeling sad because they lost their favorite device. What do you do?

    a) Offer to help them look for it.
    b) Tell them it's just a device and not a big deal.
    c) Say nothing and continue playing with your own.

4. You and your friend both want to play with the same ball. What should you do?

    a) Take turns playing with the ball.
    b) Grab it quickly before they do.
    c) Tell them they can't play with it because you
        want to.

5. Your friend made a mistake during a game and is feeling embarrassed. How do you help?

    a) Tell them it's okay, and everyone makes mistakes.
    b) Laugh and point out the mistake to others.
    c) Ignore it and keep playing.

See answer key page...

By learning to identify genuine friendships and understanding the dynamics that make them work, you're setting the stage for stronger, more fulfilling connections. And remember, the best friendships aren't just about having fun—they're about growing together, supporting each other, and enjoying the wild ride of middle school. So keep your eyes open, trust your instincts, and get ready to build a squad that'll stick with you through thick and thin.

1.2 BEYOND THE SCREEN: BUILDING REAL-LIFE CONNECTIONS IN A DIGITAL AGE

In today's hyper-connected world, where snapping, tweeting, and gaming dominate much of our social lives, it's easy to forget the power of a face-to-face conversation. Sure, sending memes back and forth can keep the laughs going, but there's something about sitting across from someone and sharing a story or a slice of pizza that just doesn't translate through a screen. It's like comparing the aroma of freshly baked cookies to a picture of cookies on your phone—both are sweet, but only one has the warmth and the mouth-watering magic.

Balancing our online interactions with real-life connections is crucial, not just for our social lives but for our emotional health, too. Think about it: when you're chatting in person, you can see the other person's expressions, their gestures, and their reactions in real-time. This isn't just useful for avoiding misunderstandings (like not realizing your text joke didn't land until it's too late), but it also helps in developing empathy. Seeing someone's face light up when you share good news or noticing their shoulders slump when they're disappointed teaches you more about human emotions than any emoji ever could.

Let's get practical here. Say you've made a friend online, someone who shares your passion for fantasy novels or your obsession with Minecraft. Transitioning this digital friendship into the real world can be awesome but also a bit daunting. Here's a safe way to go about it: arrange to meet up in a public place, maybe a library or a café, and consider bringing along a mutual friend or even a trusted adult. This isn't just about safety; it's also about easing the transition from screen to real-life scenarios, which can sometimes feel as awkward as singing without background music.

Now, what about getting even more involved in your community or school? It's one thing to comment on posts or join online groups, but active participation in local events or clubs can really anchor your social experiences. Whether it's joining the drama club, volunteering at a local charity, or signing up for a sports team, these activities allow you to connect with people who share your interests and give you a platform to express yourself outside of the digital world. And hey, the more you get involved, the more you're seen as someone who steps up—and that's a great way to naturally grow your circle of friends.

Through all these real-world interactions, you not only get to build stronger, more meaningful relationships, but you also develop skills that no online platform can teach. Skills like reading the room, offering a comforting presence, or just being a good listener—traits that make people feel valued and understood. After all, isn't that what being a friend is all about? So next time you find yourself reaching for your phone to check social media, maybe consider checking in with a friend in person instead. Who knows what adventures could come from a simple, "Hey, want to hang out after school?"

1.3 HANDLING PEER PRESSURE: SAYING NO WITH CONFIDENCE

Imagine you're at a party, and someone passes you a drink you know you shouldn't have, or your friends are urging you to skip class to hang out at the mall. Sounds familiar? That's peer pressure, a high-stakes drama that unfolds in the halls and classrooms of middle schools everywhere. Peer pressure happens when your pals, or sometimes just classmates you kinda know, push you to do something that you're not comfortable with. It can make you wear clothes you don't really like, laugh at jokes you don't find funny, or do things that make your stomach twist in knots. Why? Because fitting in feels as crucial as breathing, and standing out feels about as good as showing up to school in your pajamas.

Knowing what peer pressure is and why it happens is one thing, but dealing with it effectively is another game altogether. Picture this scenario: you're about to take a math test, and the class genius offers to let you peek at their answers. It's tempting, right? But here's where building refusal skills comes in handy. You could say something like, "No thanks, I've got this," or "I need to try this on my own." It sounds simple, but saying no with confidence can feel like lifting a hundred-pound weight off your shoulders. It takes practice. Try role-playing with a friend or even in front of a mirror. Practice makes perfect, and soon, saying no will feel as natural as acing your favorite video game.

Boosting your self-esteem is like putting on armor when you go into battle against peer pressure. When you feel good about who you are, you're less likely to change just to fit in. Let's do a quick exercise. Use the list below and write down three things you're really good at and three things you like about yourself. These can be anything from being a great listener to loving how dedicated you are to your pet hamster. This list is your reminder that you're awesome, just as you are. When peer pressure tries to tell you otherwise, this list is your shield.

3 Things	
I am good at ...	I like about me ...
①	①
②	②
③	③

Finally, remember, everyone needs a squad—a group of friends and maybe a few key adults who have your back no matter what. These are the people you can vent to when you feel like everyone is trying to push you in a direction you don't want to go. They're also the ones who will celebrate with you when you stand your ground. And here's a pro tip: sometimes, adults—like a cool aunt or your favorite teacher—can give you killer advice on how to handle tricky situations because, believe it or not, they've been where you are now.

Navigating the push and pull of what you want to do and what others want you to do is like walking a tightrope. It's all about balance. Remember, true friends will respect your choices, even if they're different from theirs. And every time you choose what's right for you, you're not just saying no to peer pressure; you're saying yes to yourself. So the next time you feel that familiar push to conform, take a deep breath, remember your awesome list, and stand your ground with a smile. It's your life, your choices, and yes, you've totally got this!

1.4 THE TRUTH ABOUT CLIQUES: NAVIGATING POPULARITY AND EXCLUSIVITY

Let's talk about cliques—the exclusive groups that seem to have their own VIP section in the cafeteria. You know the ones I'm talking about. They often have an unspoken dress code, a secret handshake, or a look that can make or break your social life (or so it seems). Cliques are like the popular brand everyone wants, but not everyone can have. Sure, they can offer a sense of belonging, but they can also make you feel like you're on the outside looking in.

Cliques form when a group of friends closes ranks, deciding either consciously or subconsciously that no one else is welcome to join their elite circle. It's like they've built a fort, and the password changes daily. The allure is undeniable; being part of a clique can feel like you've won the middle school lottery. But here's the catch: cliques often demand that you fit a certain mold. And let's be honest, who wants to be a copy when you're born to be an original?

But what if you find yourself on the outskirts, or worse, booted out of what seemed like your squad? It can feel like you're walking the plank. Here's where you need to harness your inner captain. Remember, your worth isn't determined by a group's acceptance or rejection. It's about knowing who you are and what you stand for. When faced with the pressures to conform, anchor yourself in your values and interests. Maybe you're passionate about art, coding, or sports—whatever it is, dive deep into these interests. Often, you'll find other like-minded folks who appreciate you for who you are, not for who the clique wants you to be.

Now, let's shift gears and talk strategy. How do you deal with the pressures and exclusivity of cliques? First, observe. Watch how these groups interact. Is there kindness and openness, or does it feel more like a scene from a wildlife show where only the strong survive? This can tell you a lot about whether this is a crew you'd actually want to sail with. If you decide it's not for you, that's totally fine. Look for people who share your interests and values. Start conversations in art class, join a club, or volunteer. These are all great ways to meet new friends who are more in tune with the real you.

Promoting inclusivity is like being the captain who invites everyone on deck. It's about making sure no one eats alone, that new kids feel welcome, and that different isn't just tolerated but celebrated. Have you ever noticed how a chain is only as strong as its weakest link? Well, a friend group is only as strong as its most excluded member. By choosing inclusivity, you're not just building friendships; you're building a stronger, kinder community.

Lastly, let's talk about the role of self-identity in all this. Knowing who you are, what you stand for, and where you shine can be your armor against the negative aspects of cliques. When you are secure in your identity, you are less likely to change just to fit into a group. It's like having a compass that guides you through the choppy waters of middle school social life. So, take time to get to know yourself. What are your strengths? Your passions? What makes you, well, you? These are your coordinates on the map of life, and they'll help you navigate through any social storm.

Navigating the world of cliques doesn't have to feel like a doomed voyage. With a strong sense of self and a commitment to including others, you can chart a course that's true to who you are, discovering the richer, more rewarding waters of genuine friendships. And remember, the most interesting stories aren't about fitting in —they're about standing out.

1.5 GOSSIP, RUMORS, AND HOW TO STAY ABOVE THEM

Gossip and rumors—just saying the words can make you feel like you're back in the school hallway, overhearing whispers about someone's new haircut or who got caught passing notes in class. It might seem like harmless chatter, but when the whispers are about you or someone you care about, it suddenly isn't so harmless anymore. Imagine this: one day, you're walking down the hall, and you hear people snickering behind you. Later, you find out a rumor's been spreading—a rumor that's not only untrue but also pretty hurtful. It stings, right? That's because gossip and rumors can slice through the busy hum of school life like a cold breeze, leaving confusion and hurt feelings in their wake.

So, why do people gossip? Sometimes, it's out of boredom; other times, it's a clumsy attempt to fit in or seem more interesting. But regardless of the reasons, the impact is often the same: someone ends up feeling isolated or hurt. Let's say someone spreads a rumor that a classmate cheated on a test. Whether it's true or not, that rumor can tarnish reputations and erode trust. And it's not just the person being gossiped about who feels the effects; it can sour the mood of the entire class or school, turning what should be a safe place into a theater of whispers and side-eyes.

But here's the good news—you don't have to be part of the problem. You can be the person who changes the game. When you find yourself in the middle of a gossip situation, you have choices. For starters, you can change the subject. This might sound too simple to be effective but think about it: if someone tries to dish out some juicy gossip to you about someone's embarrassing moment during gym class, steer the conversation towards something totally unrelated, like asking about the upcoming school dance or the new science project. It's like performing a magic trick—the gossip disappears!

What if changing the subject doesn't work? Sometimes, you might have to be more direct. Walking away is a powerful statement. It shows you're not interested in spreading negativity about someone else. And if you're feeling really brave, stand up for the person who's being gossiped about. Imagine the scene: someone is spreading a rumor, and you jump in with, "Hey, that doesn't sound like something they'd do. Let's not talk about them when they're not here to share their side." You've just shown there's a way to keep the conversation clean and respectful.

Promoting positive communication is like planting flowers in a garden—it beautifies the environment and encourages others to do the same. One way to do this is by practicing what you preach. Make it a habit to speak well of others or to share good news. When your friends see you making an effort to be positive, they're more likely to follow suit. And let's not forget about role-plays. These can be fun and enlightening. Grab a friend and practice scenarios where you fend off gossip, perhaps turning a potentially harmful conversation into a constructive one. It's like rehearsing for a play; the more you practice, the better you'll perform in real life.

Critical thinking is your secret weapon against rumors. It's easy to accept juicy bits of gossip as truth, especially when they're about someone you don't know well. But take a step back and think about it. Ask yourself: Where did this information come from? Is it confirmed? Could there be another side to the story? By pausing to consider these questions, you're not just avoiding spreading unverified facts; you're also building a reputation as someone who thinks before they speak. And in the swirling social world of middle school, that's a trait that can really set you apart.

Navigating the murky waters of gossip and rumors isn't just about keeping your own nose clean; it's about setting a standard for those around you. When you choose to stay above the fray, you're making a statement about the kind of friend and classmate you want to be—one who builds others up instead of tearing them down. And that's a role that can truly transform your middle school experience, turning everyday interactions into opportunities for kindness and growth. So, next time you catch a whisper or a rumor, remember you have the power to change the tune.

1.6 DEALING WITH BULLYING: PRACTICAL STEPS TO TAKE CHARGE

Let's face it, bullying is one of those ugly things no one should have to deal with, especially in school, where you're supposed to be safe and focused on learning cool new things, not dodging mean comments or worse. But it happens, and it comes in different forms—some you might recognize and some you might not. Understanding these can help you stand strong against them and support others who might be struggling silently.

So, what exactly are we up against? There's the old-school, classic bullying we see in movies—shoving, tripping, or other physical stuff, which is outright and easy to spot. But then there's verbal bullying, which can slip under the radar with mean jokes, teasing, or name-calling. And let's not forget about cyberbullying, a sneakier villain. It hides behind screens, spreading rumors, sharing embarrassing photos, or sending threatening messages online. Each type is harmful and can make school feel like walking through a minefield.

Now, if you find yourself facing any of these bullying beasts or see someone else who is, it's crucial to know how to respond. First off, document everything. Whether it's screenshots of digital nastiness or a quick note about what happened and when after someone said something hurtful, keeping a record is key. It helps adults take action because, yes, the next step is to talk to someone. A teacher, counselor, or any trusted adult at school can be your ally. They need to know what's happening to step in and help make it stop.

But what if you're seeing it happen? If you're a bystander, you've got power, too. Sometimes, just being there for someone, letting them know you've got their back, can mean the world. And if you feel safe enough, speak up. Bullies back down when they see their behavior isn't acceptable to the crowd.

Dealing with bullying is tough and no joke, but remember, it's not just about stopping the bad stuff. It's also about healing from it. If bullying has got you down, talk about it—with friends, family, counselors and youth pastors—they're all good for this. And try some activities that boost your mood and self-esteem. Whether it's sports, music, art, or just hanging out with positive people, do things that make you feel good about yourself. It's like putting armor on your self-esteem, making you stronger in the long run.

And here's where we can all start to change the game; creating a supportive community begins with each of us. Stand up for kindness. Maybe propose ideas like a 'kindness week' at school, where everyone makes an effort to be extra nice and inclusive. Projects like these can shift the whole vibe of a place, making bullying less likely to fester.

Schools can have anti-bullying campaigns or workshops where students and teachers learn about the impacts of bullying and how to handle it effectively. Imagine if every student took a stand and decided that bullying stopped with them—what a school that would be! It's about building a culture where everyone is respected and valued, and it starts with us, right here, right now.

So, keep your chin up and your eyes open, not just for yourself but for everyone around you. Stand tall, stand together, and make those school halls safer and kinder for everyone. Remember, it's not just about getting through school—it's about making it a better place for everyone while you're there. And that's something worth fighting for, don't you think?

EMOTIONAL INTELLIGENCE AND SELF-DISCOVERY

Ever had one of those days where everything feels like an emotional rollercoaster? One minute, you're laughing at a joke; the next, you're fuming over a spilled drink, and then suddenly, you're sad about a movie where the dog doesn't make it home. Welcome to the wild world of emotions in middle school, where it sometimes feels like your feelings are in the driver's seat, and oh boy, do they like to take sharp turns!

But here's some good news: getting to know your emotions isn't just about strapping in and buckling up for the ride; it's about learning how to drive. This chapter is all about tuning into your emotional world more deeply—understanding what sets off your joy buzzer or your anger alarm, boosting your self-awareness, and managing the whole colorful spectrum of your feelings. Let's explore some tools and tricks to help you navigate this vibrant inner landscape.

2.1 EMOTIONAL CHECK-INS: UNDERSTANDING YOUR FEELINGS

Recognize Emotional Triggers

First up, let's talk about emotional triggers. Imagine you're a detective in your own emotional mystery. Some things, like a surprise pop quiz or a last-minute cancellation of plans, might set off your annoyance alarm. Or maybe seeing someone alone at lunch pulls at your sadness string. Recognizing these triggers is like finding clues on what stirs up your feelings.

To get super sleuth about it, try keeping a feelings journal. No, it's not like your regular diary. It's more about jotting down what happened right before you felt a rush of emotion. Saw a friend get teased and felt angry? Write it down. Got a compliment on your project and felt proud? That goes in the journal, too. Over time, you'll start seeing patterns, like your own emotional map, which helps you predict and prepare for your reactions.

Practice Self-awareness

Now, being self-aware is like being the captain of your ship; you need to know where your vessel is heading and why. Regular check-ins with yourself, like a quick mental rundown of how you feel throughout the day, can help a lot. It's like hitting the pause button in the middle of a chaotic game and taking a moment to strategize your next move.

Why not set a few reminders on your phone or smartwatch to pause and reflect? Ask yourself, "How am I feeling right now, and why?" You might be surprised at how often you're actually feeling something mildly in the background, like a soft soundtrack to your day, without even realizing it.

Develop Emotional Vocabulary

Have you ever felt an emotion that feels too complex to describe, like when you're excited but nervous at the same time? Expanding your emotional vocabulary can help you pinpoint exactly what you're feeling. This isn't just about swapping 'sad' for 'melancholy'. It's about discovering the nuances in your emotions, which can be incredibly validating and enlightening.

Try this: next time you journal about your feelings, challenge yourself to describe your emotions without using the basic words like "happy" or "mad". Reach for deeper, more descriptive words like "elated," "irritated," or "anxious." There are tons of emotion wheels available online that can help you find the exact word you're looking for. It's like turning your emotional crayon box into a full-blown artist's palette.

Normalize Emotional Fluctuations

Here's a big one: your emotions are supposed to change. That's right, feeling moody isn't just a middle school thing; it's a human thing. One minute you're up, the next you're down, and that's perfectly normal. The key is to ride these waves gracefully, knowing that no emotion is final.

Mindfulness techniques can be absolute lifesavers here. Ever tried mindful breathing? It's like hitting the reset button on your emotional state. Just take five minutes, breathe in deeply through your nose, hold for a few seconds, and exhale slowly through your mouth. Focus only on your breath and how it feels to fill up and empty out. It's a simple way to calm the emotional storm and get back to feeling more like yourself.

So, as you step further into the labyrinth of middle school, remember: understanding your emotions isn't just about handling the ups and downs; it's about knowing yourself better. It's about ensuring you're in the driver's seat, even when the road gets bumpy. And with these tools, you'll not only know how to read your emotional map but also how to navigate it like a pro. Ready to get started? Your emotions are, and they're ready to teach you everything they know.

2.2 EMPATHY IN ACTION: RELATING TO OTHERS' EMOTIONS

Empathy is like having a superpower in your social toolkit, allowing you to connect with others on a deeper level. But what exactly is empathy? It's the ability to understand and share the feelings of another person. It's seeing the world through their eyes, even if just for a moment. Imagine you're watching a movie, and you find yourself tearing up when the main character feels sad or jumping with joy when they triumph. That's empathy—feeling with others. And guess what? Strengthening this ability can transform your relationships and make you a superhero of understanding your own life.

Stepping into Someone Else's Shoes

Let's kick off with some practical exercises to boost your empathy skills. Role-reversal scenarios are an excellent way to start. Here's how it works: team up with a friend or a family member and act out different situations where one of you is the listener and the other one shares a problem they're facing. Then, swap roles. This not only helps you understand their perspective but also gives you a peek into their emotional world. Another fun activity is perspective-taking tasks. Next time you're in a disagreement, try to argue the other person's point of view instead of your own. Sounds crazy, right? But it's a powerful way to truly grasp where they're coming from.

Mastering the Art of Active Listening

Active listening is another secret ingredient to becoming an empathy ninja. It's more than just hearing words; it's about really absorbing what the other person is saying. Here's how you can be a pro: maintain eye contact to show you're engaged, nod to signal you're following along, and paraphrase what they've said to confirm you've understood correctly. This doesn't mean staring them down or parroting their every word—show that you're with them in the conversation, not planning your lunch or zoning out.

Next time you're chatting with someone, try focusing entirely on them. Ignore that buzzing phone and the chatter around you. You might be surprised at how much more you connect when you're genuinely listening, not just waiting for your turn to speak. This not only makes the other person feel valued but also deepens your understanding of what they're experiencing.

Responding with Compassion

Now, how do you respond once you've tuned into someone's emotions? It's all about compassionate responses. These are reactions that acknowledge and validate what the other person is feeling without immediately trying to fix the problem. For example, if a friend tells you they're upset about not making the soccer team, instead of jumping in with, "Don't worry, there's always next year!" try saying, "That sounds really tough. I'd be disappointed, too." This shows you're acknowledging their feelings as valid and important.

Compassionate responses create a safe space for people to express themselves and feel understood. This doesn't mean you can't help find solutions, but it's crucial to first acknowledge what they're going through. This approach can significantly strengthen your friendships and family relationships, making you a go-to person when someone needs to talk.

Empathy in Group Settings

Empathy isn't just for one-on-one interactions; it's also super important in groups, like in class projects or sports teams. Understanding and sharing the feelings of others can make you a star team player or a group leader everyone respects. For instance, if you notice a team member feeling left out, you might encourage the group to involve them more, improving the team dynamics and everyone's experience.

Let's take a look at a famous media example, like Double Dare, to wrap our heads around this. Think about the game show where the characters have to work together to solve a problem. Notice how they often have to understand each other's fears and motivations to succeed? That's empathy in action. By bringing this into your own group activities, you can help everyone work better together, making group projects or team sports more enjoyable and successful.

So, as you move forward, think of empathy as your secret superpower. Whether you're navigating the halls of middle school, hanging out with friends, or dealing with family at home, understanding and sharing the feelings of those around you can make a huge difference. It turns everyday interactions into opportunities for connection and growth, and hey, who doesn't want to be known as the empathetic superhero in their circle?

2.3 THE CONFIDENCE FORMULA: BUILDING AND MAINTAINING YOUR SELF-ESTEEM

Building your self-esteem is like planting your very own garden. It requires patience, care, and sometimes a bit of trial and error. Think of each seed as a small goal or achievement that you're planting, and with the proper attention and environment, it'll blossom into something beautiful—aka, a healthy dose of self-confidence. Let's get our hands dirty and explore how setting achievable goals can really help your self-esteem grow.

Setting small and manageable goals is like creating a personal treasure map where X marks the spot of your success. It's not about setting out to conquer the world overnight. Instead, it's about identifying smaller, achievable tasks that you can accomplish fairly quickly. For instance, instead of saying, "I want to be the best math student in class," start with, "I will complete all my math homework on time this week." Achieving this can give you a real boost, and bit by bit, these small victories add up to big confidence. You can make this fun and trackable by creating a goal chart or a checklist in a notebook or a digital app. Every time you tick off a goal, it's like giving yourself a high-five. Before you know it, you'll start feeling more capable and confident in handling bigger challenges.

Now, let's talk about celebrating your wins. This might sound a bit like throwing yourself a party for every little thing you do, and you know what? That's exactly right! Whether you aced a quiz, stood up in front of the class without getting a jelly-legs moment, or finally nailed that skateboard trick, take a moment to really enjoy your achievement. Share your success with family or friends, do a little victory dance in your room, or treat yourself to your favorite snack. These celebrations make your achievements real and remind you of your capabilities. The trick is to recognize that no success is too small to be celebrated. Each one is a stepping stone to building stronger self-esteem.

Positive self-talk is your secret weapon in maintaining self-esteem. It's like having an internal hype-person who's always ready to cheer you on. But here's the catch—sometimes, our inner voice can be less of a cheerleader and more of a critic. Ever caught yourself thinking, "I can't do this" or "I'm not good enough"? We all have those moments. The key is to catch these negative thoughts and flip them into something positive. Instead of "I can't do this," try "I'm going to give it my best shot." Changing your self-talk requires practice, but over time, it can significantly alter how you perceive yourself. Maybe keep a journal where you write down negative thoughts and reframe them into positive affirmations. This exercise can help you become more aware of your self-talk and steer it in a direction that boosts your self-esteem.

Finding and learning from role models and mentors can turbocharge your journey to stronger self-esteem. Think about someone you admire—maybe a teacher, coach, older sibling, or even a character from a book or movie. What qualities do they possess that you respect? Is it their courage, kindness, or killer coding skills? Connecting with role models and mentors, either in real life or through stories and biographies, can provide you with a blueprint for developing your own strengths and qualities. If possible, reach out to them. Ask questions about how they overcame challenges or how they built their skills. Most people are happy to share advice and wisdom. Remember, you don't have to replicate their path, but you can certainly learn from it to carve out your own.

So, as you set out to plant your garden of goals, celebrate every bloom, nurture your self-talk, and learn from those who inspire you, watch as your garden of self-esteem flourishes. Every step you take, every goal you achieve, and every positive affirmation you repeat sows the seeds of a more confident you, ready to take on the world, one achievement at a time.

2.4 STRESS BUSTERS: TECHNIQUES TO MANAGE ANXIETY AND STRESS

Imagine this: You've got a math test tomorrow, your science project is due at the end of the week, and your best friend is mad at you for reasons unknown. Sounds like a recipe for a stress milkshake, right? Stress is like that unwelcome guest who pops up just when you think you've got your middle school life under control. But fear not! Let's unpack some cool strategies to kick stress to the curb and keep your cool like a pro.

First off, let's play detective and figure out what's really cooking up the stress stew in your life. Is it the pile of homework staring at you from your desk? Or maybe it's those moments when your family doesn't get what you're going through? Identifying your stressors is like shining a spotlight on gremlins hiding in the dark – once you see them clearly, they're a lot easier to deal with. So, grab a notebook and jot down what's bugging you throughout the week. Is it during tests, right before soccer practice, or at home when chores pile up? Knowing what flips your stress switch is a giant leap toward turning it off.

Now, onto one of the coolest tools in your stress-busting toolkit: relaxation techniques. Let's start with deep breathing exercises. It's like finding the chill button on your body's remote control. Here's how it works: find a quiet spot, sit comfortably, and take a slow, deep breath through your nose, imagining you're filling your belly with air like a balloon. Hold it briefly, then let it out through your mouth like you're gently blowing on a dandelion. Repeat a few times and feel the calm wash over you. Pretty simple, right?

But wait, there's more! Ever tried progressive muscle relaxation? It's like giving your body a mini vacation. Here's the deal: tighten a group of muscles as you breathe in, hold them for a few seconds, and then release them as you breathe out. Start from your toes and work your way up to your forehead. It's not just relaxing; it's like sending a peace treaty to every part of your body.

And for those who love a little imagination, guided imagery is like a mini-vacation for your mind. Close your eyes and picture a place where you feel happy and calm. Maybe it's a beach with waves gently lapping at the shore or a cozy nook in your room with rain tapping on the window. Let your senses dive into this place and hang out there for a while. By the time you open your eyes, you'll feel like you just returned from a stress-free zone.

Alright, moving on to something more structured: time management skills. Managing your time wisely is like having a superpower that keeps stress at bay. Start by getting to know the magical world of planners and digital apps. They're like having a personal assistant who's always got your back. Set up a schedule that's not just about homework and chores. Include time for breaks, hobbies, and hanging out with friends. Prioritize your tasks – big tests and projects obviously need a front-row seat in your planning arena. And remember, every big task can be broken down into smaller, less intimidating pieces. Tackle them one at a time, and watch your stress melt away like ice cream on a sunny day.

Lastly, let's chat about keeping your body in tip-top shape because, believe it or not, it's a huge part of keeping stress levels down. Regular physical activity is like a double-edged sword for stress. It not only boosts your mood but also helps you blow off some steam. You don't have to run marathons—just dance in your room, stretch during a TV show, or take a walk around the block. Combine this with munching on balanced meals (yes, veggies and fruits need to be more than just decorations on your plate) and catching enough Zs at night. A well-rested, well-nourished body makes a strong fortress against stress.

So, there you have it—a bunch of tools and tricks to help you manage stress like a boss. Whether it's tuning into your body's needs, organizing your time, or just taking deep breaths, remember, you've got what it takes to keep calm and carry on. And hey, next time stress tries to crash your party, you'll be more than ready to show it the door.

2.5 DISCOVERING YOUR PASSIONS: EXPLORING PERSONAL INTERESTS

Think about the last time you did something just because it was fun, and you totally lost track of time. Maybe you were sketching, coding a new app, or even organizing your room in a way that would make Marie Kondo proud. These moments are like little clues in a treasure hunt, leading you to discover your true passions. But let's be honest—sometimes, figuring out what makes your heart sing isn't all that straightforward, especially when there are a gazillion options out there. So, how about we turn this quest for passion into an exciting exploration?

Experimenting with new activities is like taste-testing at a candy store—you never know what will make your taste buds dance until you try a bunch! And the cool part? So many clubs, online courses, and local workshops are just brimming with possibilities. Always been curious about astronomy? Join a local stargazing club or sign up for an online workshop. Or maybe the mysterious world of magic tricks has you intrigued? There's probably a community class for that! The key is to step out of your comfort zone. Try coding, pottery, or even something quirky like unicycle riding. Each new activity is a potential spark for a lifelong passion, and the more you try, the more likely you are to stumble upon something that really lights you up inside.

Now, while you're dabbling in these new experiences, it's super important to pause and reflect on what feels awesome. Remember that time you helped organize the school carnival, and it felt like a significant win? Or when you figured out a challenging math problem and felt like a genius? These aren't just random extraordinary moments but signposts pointing toward your passions. Reflecting on these experiences helps you connect the dots. It could be leading events that excite you or solving puzzles that light up your brain. Whatever it is, these reflections help you understand more about what makes you tick. So, grab a notebook and start jotting down what activities make you feel alive, which ones you're good at, and which ones you could totally do without. This isn't just busy work; it's your personal roadmap to a passionate life.

Connecting with like-minded folks can turn your passion from a solo adventure into a shared journey. Whether it's joining a club at school, finding a community online, or even starting your own group, there's strength and inspiration in numbers. Imagine being part of a photography club where everyone is as shutter-happy as you, sharing tips, challenging each other, and exploring new angles together. Or maybe you find an online community of writers where you can share your stories, get feedback, and geek out about plot twists. These connections can be a major boost, not just for your skills but also for keeping your enthusiasm high. Plus, it's always more fun to explore your passions with buddies who get just as excited about them as you do.

And here's the real magic trick: weaving your passions into your daily life. It's one thing to discover what you love doing; it's another to make it a part of your everyday routine. Say you've discovered a love for drawing. Why not start a comic strip for the school newspaper? Or use your art skills to jazz up your class presentations? Integrating your passions into your daily activities doesn't just make the mundane more enjoyable; it also gives you more time to do what you love, making every day a little brighter. When it comes to schoolwork, linking your interests can make learning a whole lot more engaging. Writing an essay on the French Revolution? Add a twist by analyzing the art from that era, combining history with your love for art.

So, as you set out on this quest to uncover and nurture your passions, remember that it's all about exploration, reflection, connection, and integration. Each step is a piece of the puzzle, and when you start putting them together, you're not just building a hobby; you're building a happier, more fulfilled you. Dive into new experiences, reflect on what brings you joy, connect with others who share your interests, and find ways to make your passions a part of your everyday life. Who knows? What starts as a fun activity could turn into a lifelong passion or even a future career. But for now, just enjoy the ride and see where it takes you. After all, the thrill is in the discovery.

2.6 SETTING PERSONAL GOALS: A GUIDE TO ACHIEVING WHAT MATTERS TO YOU

Hey there! Let's talk about setting goals. Not just any goals, but the kind that actually sticks. You know, the ones that don't just evaporate two weeks into trying something new. We're diving into the world of SMART goals—those are Specific, Measurable, Achievable, Relevant, and Time-bound. These aren't just fancy words; they're your new best friends in the realm of getting things done.

So, imagine you're aiming to boost your math grades. Instead of just saying, "I want to be better at math," which is pretty vague and floaty, a SMART goal would be, "I will improve my math grade from a B to an A by the end of the semester by studying for an extra hour every Tuesday and Thursday evening." See the difference? It's specific and has a clear timeline, making it way easier to stick to.

Now, let's break it down. Specific is the 'what, why, and how' of your goals. Measurable means you can track your progress and know when you've hit your target. Achievable is about setting goals that are challenging yet possible. Relevant ensures your goals align with your bigger dreams, and Time-bound means setting a deadline. This way, goals aren't just wishes but actionable steps you can check off your list.

To create a SMART chart, we need to define a goal using the SMART framework, which stands for **Specific, Measurable, Achievable, Relevant, and Time-bound**. Here's a template for how a SMART goal chart could be structured:

Example SMART Goal: "Improve Math Grades by 15% in the Next Semester"

SMART Criteria*Details**

Specific Improve math grades by 15%.

Measurable Compare current math grades with grades at the end of the semester.

Achievable With 1 hour of extra math tutoring and practice every day.

Relevant Math is a core subject needed for academic success.

Time-bound Achieve this goal by the end of the upcoming semester.

You can now fill in the blanks with your specific goal details to create your personalized SMART goal.

SMART Goals

S	**Specific** What am I going to do? Why is this important to me?
M	**Measurable** How will I measure my success? How will I know when I have achieved my goal?
A	**Attainable** What will I do to achieve this goal? How will I accomplish this goal?
R	**Relevant** Is this goal worthwhile? How will achieving it help me? Does this goal fit my values?
T	**Time-Bound** When will I accomplish my goal? How long will I give myself?

But here's the real game-changer: breaking those big, hairy goals into smaller chunks. Let's stick with the math example. Say your big goal is to ace the final exam. Start by setting mini-goals like finishing all your homework on time each week, attending after-school help sessions twice a month, or mastering one new concept every week. These bite-sized goals are like stepping stones. They build up your confidence and skills gradually, so by the time the exam rolls around, you're ready to knock it out of the park.

Keeping an eye on your progress is key. Ever heard of a goal-tracking app? These nifty tools are perfect for keeping your goals front and center. You can see your progress in real-time, which is super motivating. Plus, if you notice you're slipping off track, you can adjust your plans without missing a beat. It's like having a coach in your pocket, cheering you on, and giving you a nudge when you need it.

And here comes the fun part—celebrating your milestones! Every time you hit one of your mini-goals, do something to celebrate. It could be something small like treating yourself to your favorite snack or taking a half-hour extra screen time. These celebrations aren't just rewards but reminders that you're making real progress. They fuel your journey, keeping you pumped about reaching that next milestone.

Setting goals the SMART way turns your hopes into realities. It's like building a bridge to your dreams. You start on one side with a wish, and step by step; you make your way across until, before you know it, you're there, looking back at how far you've come. And the view? Absolutely worth it.

So, grab your planner or fire up that app and start plotting your path to awesomeness. Whether it's acing a test, getting better at a sport, or learning a new skill, remember to break it down, track your progress, and celebrate every win. You've got this, and with SMART goals in your toolkit, you're ready to turn your dreams into your reality.

As we wrap up this chapter on setting personal goals, remember the power lies in your hands. The journey of achieving what matters to you is paved with commitment and the right strategies. By setting SMART goals, breaking them into manageable steps, monitoring your progress, and celebrating your successes, you're not just chasing your dreams—you're living them. These steps are your building blocks for success not just in school but in life. So, dream big, set your goals smartly, and take one step at a time. There's no telling how far you'll go!

Ready to turn the page? In the next chapter, we'll explore how to navigate the challenges and triumphs of academic life, setting you up for success inside the classroom and beyond. Let's keep this momentum going!

ACADEMIC STRATEGIES FOR SUCCESS

Ever felt like your school life is a wild jungle, filled with the beasts of homework, projects, and never-ending tests, all lurking around waiting to pounce? Well, you're not alone in this wilderness! And guess what? There's a way to tame these wild beasts and maybe even make them your pals. It's all about mastering the art of organizing your school life. Think of it as being the Indiana Jones of your academic adventure. Cool, right? Let's gear up, grab our maps (or planners, in this case), and figure out how to navigate this exciting terrain without losing our hats!

3.1 ORGANIZING YOUR SCHOOL LIFE: TIME MANAGEMENT TIPS

Prioritize Tasks Like a Pro

First up, let's talk about prioritizing your tasks. Imagine your school tasks are like a bunch of wildberries you've gathered. Some are super sweet and need to be eaten right away (urgent!), while others can wait a bit before they go bad (not so urgent). Prioritizing is all about figuring out which berries to eat first so none goes to waste. This means deciding which assignments to tackle in the school jungle based on how urgent and important they are. An excellent tool to help with this is the priority matrix—a simple chart that lets you sort your tasks into categories: urgent and important, important but not urgent, urgent but not important, and neither urgent nor important. This way, you can easily see what needs your immediate attention and what can chill out for a bit.

Planner Power

Next, let's swing into the world of planners. Whether you're a fan of old-school paper planners or slick digital apps, these are your compasses in the academic jungle. They help you keep track of assignments, tests, and extracurricular activities. Setting up your planner effectively is like setting up camp: you need a clear view of everything that's going on. Start by jotting down all your deadlines and commitments. Then, break down bigger tasks into smaller steps and spread them out over the days or weeks leading up to the deadline. This way, you're not cramming all the action into one night (we've all been there, and it's no picnic!).

Routine, Routine, Routine

Establishing a routine is like setting up safe paths to navigate through the jungle. It keeps you from stumbling into quicksand or getting lost among the trees. A solid routine for school, homework, activities, and yes, even fun and relaxation can seriously reduce stress. Try to start and end your homework at the same time each day, and make sure you carve out time for breaks and leisure activities, too. It's about balancing the trek with some good old rest by the campfire.

The Battle Against Procrastination

Now, for the sneaky snake in the grass: procrastination. It's easy to put off tasks, especially when they feel like a giant boulder blocking your path. But here's a trick—break that boulder into smaller rocks. Set small, achievable goals and use a timer to do short, focused bursts of work, known as the Pomodoro Technique. Work for, say, 25 minutes, then take a 5-minute break. This method keeps your brain fresh and your motivation fueled. Also, make sure your study environment is helping, not hindering you. A clean, organized desk with minimal distractions sets the stage for a successful treasure hunt.

Visual Element: The Priority Matrix

To help you visualize how to prioritize tasks effectively, here's a simple chart called the priority matrix. It's divided into four quadrants:

- **Urgent and Important:** Tasks that need immediate attention (e.g., a project due tomorrow).
- **Important but Not Urgent:** Tasks that are important but can wait a bit (e.g., a paper due in two weeks).
- **Urgent but Not Important:** Tasks that don't contribute much to your goals but need to be done soon (e.g., some regular homework).
- **Neither Urgent nor Important:** Tasks that might not need to be done at all (e.g., reorganizing your binder for the fifth time this week).

Urgent **&** Important	Important but **Not** Urgent
Urgent but **Not** Important	**Not** Urgent or Important

This chart is your map to managing your tasks more efficiently, ensuring you use your energy and time in the smartest way possible in this wild jungle of school life.

Navigating through your academic jungle with these strategies helps you keep up with your tasks and makes the journey a lot more enjoyable and less stressful. Remember, every explorer needs a good map, a solid plan, and the right tools. With these time management tips, you're well-equipped to take on whatever the wild world of middle school throws at you. So, keep your planners updated, your priorities straight, and your adventures grand. Let's make this school year an epic expedition!

3.2 STUDY SMARTER, NOT HARDER: TECHNIQUES FOR EFFECTIVE LEARNING

Let's face it, studying can sometimes feel like trying to fill a leaky bucket—you keep pouring in information, but it just seems to slip right out. But what if I told you that there are ways to patch up that bucket and make everything stick? That's right, it's all about studying smarter, not harder. So, grab your mental duct tape, and let's patch up your study strategies with some cool techniques that actually work.

Active Learning Strategies: Your Study Superpowers

First up, let's supercharge your study sessions with some active learning strategies. These aren't just about reading your notes over and over until your eyes glaze over. No, these are about getting involved with the material, making it stick like that one catchy song you can't get out of your head. For starters, try summarizing the information in your own words. After reading a chapter, close the book and tell your cat, your mom, or even your mirror what you just learned. The act of rephrasing information cements it way better than just reading it quietly.

Next, why not teach someone else? Grab a study buddy and explain a concept to them. They say you never really know something until you can teach it, and it's true! When you're the one doing the teaching, you have to sort out your thoughts clearly, spot any gaps in your own understanding, and fill them. Plus, it's a win-win because your study buddy gets to learn, too.

And when you need to memorize facts, dates, or processes, mnemonic devices are like magic spells for your memory. Create a silly acronym, rhyme, or even form a bizarre mental image linking the bits of information. The weirder, the better because our brains love odd stuff. Remember, it's all about making the material as engaging and interactive as possible so it sticks better than your favorite brand of glue.

Study= <u>S</u>tudy <u>T</u>he <u>U</u>nforgetable <u>D</u>ata <u>Y</u>ourself The sillier the better!

Stay focused

Take breaks

Understand the material

Do your best

You've got this!

Dive Into a Pool of Diverse Resources

Now, let's talk about your study tool kit. Depending on the day, you could use a hammer, a screwdriver, or a pair of pliers. Similarly, using various study resources can help you tackle different subjects and topics more effectively. Sure, textbooks are your bread and butter, but what about mixing in some online videos for that extra flavor? Platforms like Khan Academy or CrashCourse can turn a boring topic into an adventure in minutes.

Educational apps are another great addition to your toolkit. They can turn review sessions into interactive games or quizzes, making the repetition part of studying more fun and less of a chore. And let's not forget about good old-fashioned peer study groups. Getting together with classmates can provide new insights and explanations, helping clarify tough concepts you might need help with. Plus, it's a chance to see how others organize and understand the same material, which can inspire new ways for you to approach it.

Note-Taking: Your Map Through the Knowledge Jungle

Moving on to one of the most underrated study skills ever: note-taking. But not just any note-taking—effective note-taking. It's like drawing a map as you journey through the dense jungle of information. Without it, you might remember the big landmarks but miss out on the cool, hidden paths in between. Let's explore a couple of methods that could revolutionize the way you jot things down.

The Cornell method, for instance, is fantastic for organizing your notes clearly and concisely.

You divide your paper into three sections:

- A narrow column on the left for key terms or questions
- A larger right-hand column for detailed notes
- A summary at the bottom

This setup keeps your notes neat and supports your review sessions, making it easy to quiz yourself and recap the main points.

Mind mapping, on the other hand, is perfect for visual learners. Start with the main concept in the center and draw branches out to related ideas using keywords, images, or even doodles. This method turns a boring list of notes into a vibrant, visual web of knowledge, helping you see connections between concepts and enhancing your understanding and memory.

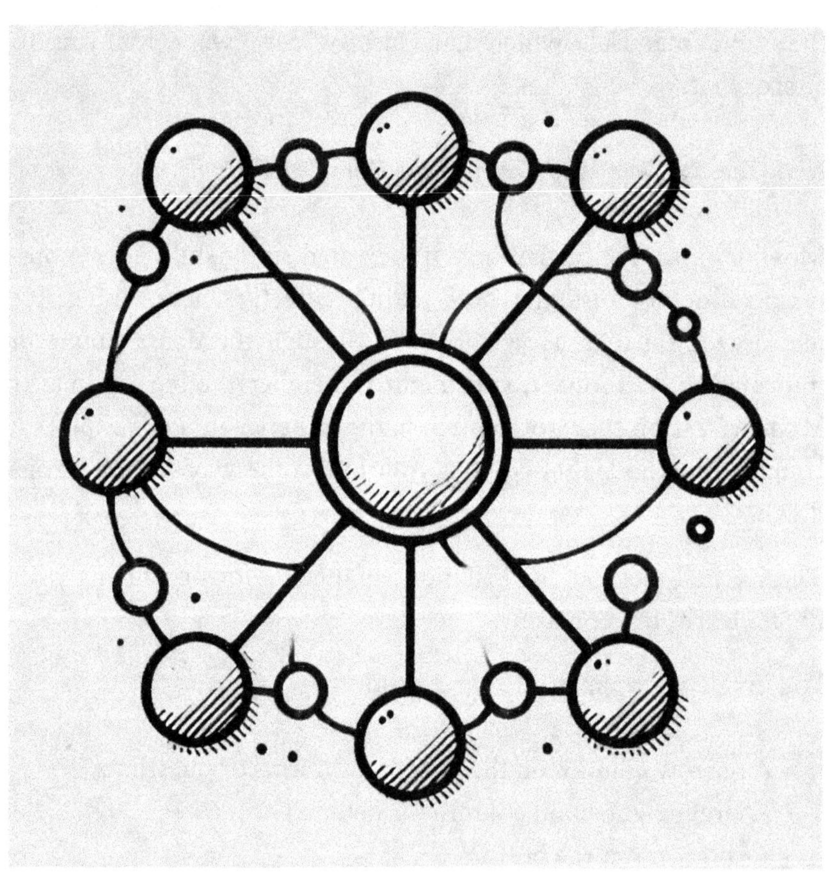

Regular Review Sessions: The Secret Ingredient to Long-Term Retention

Lastly, let's lock all that knowledge in with regular review sessions. Cramming might seem like a good idea at the time, but it's about as effective as trying to catch rain with a sieve—most of it slips right through. Instead, embrace the power of spaced repetition. This technique involves reviewing the material over increasing intervals of time. It's like watering a plant at just the right intervals to make it grow.

Start by reviewing your notes within 24 hours after learning the material to reinforce what you've just covered. Then, revisit them a few days later and again the following week. Each review session reinforces the pathways in your brain, making your recall sharper and more reliable. It's like laying down layers of varnish on a painting—you're protecting and enhancing your masterpiece of knowledge.

By integrating these techniques into your study habits, you're not just surviving the academic jungle; you're thriving in it. From active engagement with the material to varied resources, effective note-taking, and strategic reviews, each step builds on the last, forming a comprehensive, dynamic approach to learning. So, keep these tools handy and watch as studying transforms from a dreaded chore to an exciting part of your educational adventure.

3.3 HANDLING HOMEWORK: BALANCING SCHOOL AND FREE TIME

Let's face it, juggling homework and free time can sometimes feel like trying to keep a dozen ping-pong balls in the air. You want to ace your assignments but also have time to chill and enjoy life, right? Setting up a realistic homework schedule is like having a secret playbook that helps you manage all those bouncing balls without losing your cool. Here's the scoop: start by mapping out your week. Grab a calendar (digital or old-school paper works fine) and first block out times for school, meals, and enough sleep —gotta keep the engine running smoothly! Now, look at the gaps. These are your golden hours.

Divide these free slots into homework time and break time. Yes, breaks are mandatory! They're like those little rest stops on a long road trip—essential to stretch and refresh. Aim to sprinkle short breaks every 30 minutes or so during your study sessions. It keeps your brain fresh and ready to soak up more info. Remember, it's a marathon, not a sprint. Maybe set specific days for specific subjects based on your weekly workload. Got a math test on Friday? Dedicate more time to algebra on Wednesday and Thursday. This way, you're not just randomly flipping through textbooks but attacking your homework with a plan.

Now, let's talk about your homework command center—your study space. Having a dedicated spot where you hit the books can seriously boost your focus and productivity. Find a quiet corner in your home that's comfortable but not too cozy (you know, not the comfy couch where naps happen). Ensure it's well-lit and has all your study supplies at arm's reach. This is your homework haven. Personalize it with cool, inspiring stuff like motivational quotes or a funny bobble-head, whatever makes you smile. The key is to make this space distraction-free. So, bye-bye, noisy siblings and pinging phones.

Speaking of distractions, let's tackle the king of them all—our screens. Managing screen time is crucial, not just for keeping your homework on track but also for ensuring you get enough shut-eye. Too much screen time before bed can turn your sleep quality into a bit of a nightmare. Try using apps that limit your phone or tablet use during study hours. Set it to block your favorite social media apps while hitting the books. This way, you won't accidentally spend an hour on TikTok when you are supposed to be conjugating verbs.

And since we're in the business of making your homework time as efficient as possible, let's remember to tackle the tough stuff first. Dive into the most challenging or least appealing tasks when you're fresh. It's tempting to start with the easy stuff, but knocking out the big, scary assignments first can give you a massive boost of relief and confidence. Plus, everything else will seem more manageable in comparison. Break these big monsters into smaller tasks so they seem manageable. Got a massive project? Start with the research part, then move on to outlining, followed by a rough draft. Before you know it, you'll put the finishing touches on a masterpiece.

By creating a solid homework schedule, setting up a dedicated study space, managing your screen time, and tackling the most challenging assignments first, you're setting yourself up for a smoother ride through the school year. Balancing homework and free time doesn't have to be a circus act. With these strategies in place, you can keep those ping-pong balls in the air and have a hand free to grab a snack. So, gear up, get organized, and turn those potential homework hassles into victories.

3.4 PREPARING FOR TESTS: STRATEGIES THAT WORK

Alright, let's talk about the big one—test day. Whether it's a pop quiz or a final exam, tests can feel like giant, scary monsters lurking at the end of your textbook. But don't worry, I've got some tricks up my sleeve to help you tame these beasts and maybe even become friends with them. So, grab your adventurer's hat, and let's decode the mysteries of different test formats and how you can ace them!

Understanding the Terrain: Different Test Formats

First, knowing what questions to expect can make a big difference. Think of it like knowing if you're facing a dragon or a troll—you need different strategies for each! Multiple-choice questions are like puzzles; you need to pick the one right piece out of several. The trick here is to eliminate the obviously wrong answers first, which often leaves you with fewer options and a better chance of guessing right if needed. True/false questions are all about spotting the details—pay attention to absolutes like "always" or "never," which can often signal a false statement.

Then there are essay questions, like open invitations to show off what you know—but also a pitfall if you're unprepared. These require a clear plan. Start by quickly outlining your main points. Make sure you answer the question right at the beginning, then use your outline to build your argument step by step. It's like constructing a tower; you need a solid foundation and a clear structure so it doesn't topple over.

Crafting Your Battle Plan: Test Preparation Timeline

Now, let's map out your preparation timeline. Just like you wouldn't hike up a mountain without preparing, you shouldn't walk into a test without a plan. About two weeks before your test, start reviewing the material. This is your base camp, where you get acclimated and review the landscape. Use this time for a thorough review, going over notes, essays, and your previous quizzes.

One week before the test, switch to practice mode. Take practice tests if you can find them, or make your own based on your notes and homework. This is like doing a few practice climbs before the big ascent—it helps you get used to the conditions and identify any tricky spots.

The night before the test, ease up. Think of it as preparing for launch day. Review your notes briefly, but then give yourself time to relax. Listen to some music, do some light reading, or practice some relaxation techniques. It's all about getting your mind and body into the best shape for tomorrow's journey.

Keeping Your Cool: Managing Test Anxiety

Feeling a bit jittery before a test is totally normal, but let's make sure those nerves don't hijack your hard work. Deep breathing exercises can be a game-changer. Try breathing in slowly while counting to four, holding it for a count of four, then exhaling for four. It helps reset your stress response and keeps your brain getting the oxygen it loves.

Visualization techniques are also incredibly powerful. Picture yourself walking into the test, sitting down, acing every question, and walking out with a smile. It's like rehearsing a perfect performance in your mind's theater.

And don't forget about positive affirmations. These are little cheers you can tell yourself to boost your confidence. Phrases like "I am prepared, and I will do my best" can really help set a positive mindset as you step into the exam room.

Learning from the Battle: Post-Test Review

After the test, it's tempting to just move on and not think about it again. But there's a valuable treasure to be found in reviewing how you did. Take some time to go over your test once it's returned to you. Look at what questions you missed and try to figure out why. Was it because you didn't understand the material? Did you misread the question? Or maybe you ran out of time? Understanding where you went off the path helps you adjust your strategies for next time.

Also, pay attention to the questions you got right, especially if you were unsure about them. Analyzing these can reinforce what strategies worked and boost your confidence. Remember, every test, whether aced or not so much, is a chance to learn and improve.

By understanding the different types of test questions, crafting a detailed preparation timeline, managing test anxiety, and reviewing your performance afterward, you're setting yourself up not just to survive the test but to conquer it. So, keep these strategies in your toolkit, and you'll be ready to turn any test from a feared foe into a valuable ally on your academic adventure.

3.5 GROUP PROJECTS: COLLABORATING SUCCESSFULLY WITH CLASSMATES

Ah, group projects! They can either be a thrilling adventure where you discover new friendships and learn a ton, or they can feel like you're trying to herd a bunch of cats while blindfolded. It all comes down to how well your group functions as a team. Let's dive into the nitty-gritty of making your group project a smashing success, not a stress mess!

First things first, defining clear roles and responsibilities in your group is like assigning positions in a basketball game—everyone needs to know whether they're shooting hoops or guarding the basket. Right at the start, sit down with your group and discuss everyone's strengths and interests. Maybe you're a whiz at research, while your buddy is a PowerPoint guru. Assign roles that play to each member's strengths so everyone feels valuable and engaged. This clarity prevents those moments where everyone thought someone else was doing the task, and now it's due tomorrow, and nobody did it—yep, we've all been there!

Now, onto the glue that holds your group together: communication. Regular check-ins are a must. These don't have to be formal; a quick chat at the end of class or a brief online meeting can do the trick. The key is to keep everyone updated on progress and any roadblocks. Think of it as a quick team huddle where everyone shares updates, and you make sure no one's stuck or overwhelmed. And hey, feedback is a two-way street. Make sure to give and receive constructive feedback in a friendly, helpful manner. Instead of saying, "Your part of the slideshow doesn't make any sense," try, "I think your section could be even clearer if you add some bullet points or a diagram." It's all about helping each other improve, not pointing fingers.

Conflicts? Yeah, they're probably going to happen. Maybe it's about who does what, or perhaps someone feels their ideas aren't being heard. It's all part of the group project territory. Here's where you whip out your conflict resolution skills. First, stay calm and cool. Approach any disagreement with the goal of finding a solution, not winning an argument. Listen to all sides—it's amazing how many conflicts are just misunderstandings. When needed, be ready to compromise. Maybe you really wanted to do the research part, but so does someone else. Could you split it? Or maybe tackle another important section? Finding a middle ground shows you're all about the team's success, not just your own preferences.

And lastly, let's talk tools—no, not hammers and nails, but project management tools that can seriously up your group project game. Tools like Google Docs for collaborating on reports, Trello or Asana for tracking tasks, or even a shared calendar for deadlines can keep everyone on the same page. Think of these tools as your project command center where everyone can see what's happening, who's doing what, and when things are due. It's like having a map in the middle of a treasure hunt—it keeps you from wandering off into the weeds.

Navigating a group project with clear roles, effective communication, sharp conflict resolution skills, and handy management tools turns a potential nightmare into a dream team adventure. It's about leveraging each other's strengths, keeping the lines of communication wide open, and using the right tools to keep everything running smoothly. So, gear up, get organized, and get ready to make your next group project not just successful but also a great chance to connect, collaborate, and create something cool together. Remember, together, you're stronger—and hey, it's more fun that way too!

3.6 SEEKING HELP: WHEN AND HOW TO ASK FOR IT

Hey, ever felt like you're in a maze, trying to find your way out, but every turn seems just a bit more confusing? That's schoolwork sometimes, right? Well, guess what? Asking for help isn't just okay; it's actually super smart. Let's unpack the toolbox for getting the help you need, ensuring you can navigate those tricky school challenges like a pro.

Recognize the Need for Help

First, let's talk about recognizing when you might need a helping hand. It's like being on a hike and realizing you might be lost. You could wander around, hoping to find the right path, or you could pull out your map and compass, ask for help, and get back on track fast. So, how do you know it's time to ask? Your grades may not be what you hoped despite giving it your all. Or the stress of trying to figure out calculus or Shakespeare on your own is starting to feel like you're carrying a backpack full of rocks. These are your signs, your indicators that it's time to reach out.

Remember, it's totally normal to need help. It doesn't mean you're not awesome at other things. It just means you're human, and like all humans, you're learning how to navigate new territories. Recognizing this need shows you're wise and mature enough to understand that everyone, at some point, needs a little guidance.

Approaching Teachers: Crafting Your Game Plan

Now, let's strategize on how to approach your teachers. Think of it as planning how to talk to a coach when you want to improve your game. Teachers are there to guide you, but they're not mind readers, so you need to be clear about what you're struggling with.

Before you approach them, take a minute to jot down what specific areas are giving you trouble. Is it the weird symbols in algebra that seem like hieroglyphs? Or the way Shakespeare never seems to say anything straight? Having this info ready shows your teacher you're serious about learning and makes it easier for them to help you effectively.

When you talk to your teacher, be open and honest. Let them know you're committed to doing better and just need some pointers on how to get there. Most teachers will jump at the chance to help a student who's genuinely interested in learning. And remember, this isn't a one-and-done deal. Keep the communication lines open, and don't be afraid to ask follow-up questions or for additional resources.

Utilizing Tutoring Resources: Expanding Your Support Network

Sometimes, you might need more help than what your teacher can offer during school hours. That's where tutoring resources come into play. Many schools have tutoring centers where older students or teachers hang out, ready to help with almost any subject. It's like having a study buddy who knows the ropes.

Don't overlook online resources, either. There are tons of educational sites that offer tutorials, practice exercises, and even live help. And let's not forget about peer tutoring. Maybe you're a whiz at history but struggle with math, while your friend is a math genius but can't remember historical dates to save their life. Why not trade skills? You help them with the Civil War, and they help you with quadratic equations. It's a win-win.

Asking for Help Is a Strength

Most importantly, understand that asking for help is a sign of strength, not weakness. It shows you're taking charge of your learning journey, and you're determined to succeed no matter what obstacles pop up. Think of it like a video game. Sometimes, you need to find a strategy guide or ask for tips to get past a challenging level. Does that make you any less of a gamer? Nope! It just means you're smart enough to do what it takes to win.

So, remember, whether it's reaching out to a teacher, using tutoring resources, or swapping help with a friend, seeking assistance is a strategic move on your path to academic success. It's about building a support network, gathering your tools, and tackling each challenge head-on. With the right help, you can overcome any academic obstacle, turning those confusing mazes into straight paths toward your goals.

As we wrap up this chapter on navigating the complexities of school life—from managing your time and homework to acing your tests and projects—it's clear that the journey through middle school is all about learning, growing, and sometimes asking for help. Each strategy and tool we've explored is a stepping stone to becoming a more effective, confident, and happy student. So, apply these lessons, and watch as you transform challenges into achievements.

Up next, we dive into the digital world in Chapter 4, where we'll decode the secrets to balancing online and offline life—a crucial skill for any savvy middle schooler in today's connected world. Get ready to discover how to stay smart, safe, and balanced in the digital jungle!

Middle school can be a whirlwind, but guess what? You're not alone! **The Only Middle School Survival Guide You'll Ever Need** is like a friendly map that helps students ages 11-14 navigate the twists and turns of middle school life. Whether you're feeling unsure about new friends, nervous about social media, or just trying to get those homework assignments in on time—this guide has got your back.

This book is packed with real-life tips and strategies that make tackling middle school not just doable but fun. You'll learn how to build confidence, manage your emotions, and find your way through the challenges of being a tween in today's world.

But here's where *YOU* come in. Reviews are super important for families and educators when they're deciding which books can help students. Your review could be the key that helps another student thrive in middle school!

By leaving a review, you can:

- Help one more student feel confident about their first day.
- Equip a parent with tools that make their child's school experience easier.
- Provide teachers and administrators with resources to support their students better.

It only takes a minute to write a review, but it could change someone's middle school journey. Want to help out? Just scan the QR code below and leave a review today!

Thank you so much for being a part of this journey with us!

DebbieAnn Lewis

ONLINE AND OFFLINE BALANCE

Welcome to the digital jungle! It's like your regular jungle, but instead of vines, we've got charging cables, and instead of parrots, we have tweets. Navigating this online world is a big part of your daily life, right? From Snapchat streaks to endless TikTok scrolls, it's a whirlwind. But hold onto your hats because we're about to turn you into savvy explorers of this digital terrain, balancing the online buzz with your offline life. Let's jump right in!

4.1 NAVIGATING SOCIAL MEDIA RESPONSIBLY

Understand Social Media Influence

Let's start by peeling back the curtain on how social media can really mess with your emotions without noticing. Picture this: one minute, you're laughing at a goofy cat video, and the next, you're feeling bummed out because everyone seems to be having more fun than you. Social media platforms are like highlight reels—

people only post their best moments, which isn't always the full story. It's easy to feel like you're missing out or not measuring up, which can really take a toll on your self-esteem.

To stay on top of your social media game, think of it as navigating a tricky video game level. You need to recognize when it's messing with your mood. If you find yourself feeling sad, jealous, or anxious after scrolling, it might be time to take a break and do something that makes you feel good offline—like shooting hoops, drawing, or just jamming to your favorite tunes. Remember, it's okay to disconnect and remind yourself that real life isn't as picture-perfect as it seems on Instagram.

Promote Positive Posting Habits

Now, let's move on to how you can spread some good vibes online. Before you post, pause and ask yourself: Is this kind, true, and necessary? Think of each post as a digital footprint you leave behind—once it's out there, it's out there for good. So, make it something positive! Whether it's a supportive comment on a friend's post, sharing a fun memory, or posting a picture from your latest adventure, keep it upbeat and genuine.

Spreading positivity not only makes others feel good but it comes back to you, too. It's like throwing a boomerang of smiles—you send one out, and it's bound to come back your way. Fostering a positive online environment can set the tone for how others interact with your posts. Lead by example, and watch the good vibes multiply!

Recognize and Avoid Misinformation

Here's a biggie—misinformation. It spreads faster than a wildfire in the digital woods. With so much information at your fingertips, it's crucial to become a detective of what's true and what's not. Always double-check the facts before you share something. Look at credible sources, and if you're unsure, a quick fact-check on reliable news sites or educational platforms can save you from spreading false news.

Teaching others about this can also help put out the fires of misinformation. If you see a friend sharing something iffy, gently point them towards the facts. It's not about calling them out but helping them (and your circle) stay informed and savvy. Think of it as helping your friend navigate through a thick fog with a trusty flashlight.

Setting Personal Boundaries

Lastly, let's set some boundaries. Your online world should have limits, just like in real life. Decide how much time you want to spend on social media daily and stick to it. Maybe even schedule 'no-scroll' times, especially during family meals or before bed. Tell your friends about your 'online hours'—they'll understand that you're trying to balance your digital and real-life adventures. And respect their boundaries, too; if they're not replying right away, give them space. Everyone's trying to manage their own digital jungle, after all.

Setting these boundaries isn't just about reducing screen time; it's about enhancing the quality of your real life. You should have more face-to-face interactions, more time for hobbies, and yes, even more time to just be bored. Sometimes, great ideas come from moments of boredom—it's like letting your brain breathe and stretch its imaginative muscles.

Navigating social media responsibly, positively, and savvy can transform your online experience from a potential minefield into a treasure trove of connections, learning, and fun. Remember, the digital world is part of your reality but not the whole picture. Keeping a healthy balance is critical to enjoying your online and offline life, ensuring that you stay connected in the best possible ways. So, use these strategies to master the digital jungle, making it a place of positivity, truth, and respect, all while keeping your feet firmly planted in the amazing real world around you.

4.2 CYBERBULLYING: RECOGNIZING AND RESPONDING

Let's talk about something super important—cyberbullying. It's like the invisible monster lurking behind screens, and it can be really tough to spot until it's right in your face. Cyberbullying happens when someone uses digital tools, like social media, texts, or websites, to harass, threaten, or embarrass someone else. It's not just a mean comment or two; it's a persistent, ugly behavior that can make the online world feel really hostile. So, how do you know if it's happening? Well, if you or someone you know starts feeling anxious or upset after being online, or if there are direct messages (DMs) that include threats, spreading rumors, or sharing embarrassing photos without consent, bingo—that might be cyberbullying.

Here's the deal on what to do if those digital clouds start to gather. First off, document everything. Take screenshots, save texts, emails —whatever you can that shows what's going on. It's like gathering evidence; you might not need it right away, but it's good to have it just in case things escalate and you need to show an adult what's been happening.

Speaking of adults, knowing when to bring them into the game is key. Cyberbullying can sometimes get really intense, and that's when looping in a trusted adult—like a parent, teacher, or school counselor—can really help. They can offer advice and support and sometimes step in to stop the bullying if it gets out of hand. But here's the thing, don't retaliate. I know it's tempting to fire back a zinger or two, but that often just throws fuel on the fire and makes things worse. The goal is to get the bullying to stop, not to start a full-blown online war.

Finding Emotional Support

After dealing with something as tough as cyberbullying, tapping into some emotional support is like finding a calm port after a stormy sail. Talking things over can really help lighten the load. Reach out to friends who make you feel safe and supported. Share your feelings, and let them help you laugh, distract you, or give you a pep talk. Sometimes, just voicing what's bothering you can take away a lot of its power.

And don't forget about professional counselors. These folks are like emotional wizards; they know tricks to banish the blues and can give you tools to protect your feelings if bullies try to zap them. Schools usually have counselors who know all about how to deal with cyberbullying, and they can be natural allies when you're feeling stuck or scared.

Promote Digital Citizenship

Okay, so how about we all try to make the online world a better place? Promoting digital citizenship is about encouraging everyone to use the internet responsibly and kindly. Think of it as the Golden Rule of the Internet: Treat others as you want to be treated online. This means no spreading rumors, sharing embarrassing photos of others, or sending mean messages, even if you're just joking.

Being a good digital citizen also means standing up for others. If you see someone being bullied online, send them a supportive message, or if it feels safe, call out the bullying. A simple "Hey, that's not cool" can make a big difference. And always, always think before you click. Before you post, comment, or share, please take a moment to think about how it might affect others. Could it hurt someone's feelings? Could it embarrass them? If there's any doubt, maybe give that post a pass.

Navigating the online world safely and kindly isn't just about dodging the bad stuff; it's about spreading good vibes and supporting each other. By understanding the signs of cyberbullying, knowing how to respond, and promoting a positive online environment, you're not just protecting yourself; you're helping build a safer, friendlier internet for everyone. So let's keep those digital skies clear and full of good stuff because everyone deserves to have a good time online, including you!

4.3 DIGITAL FOOTPRINTS: UNDERSTANDING YOUR ONLINE PRESENCE

Have you ever thought about what happens to all those posts, comments, and likes you sprinkle across the internet? Well, they stick around, creating what's known as your digital footprint.

Imagine every time you go online, you're walking through digital sand, leaving footprints behind. Like in real sand, these prints can tell someone a lot about where you've been and what you've done. Now, why should you care? Because these tracks pile up and can influence everything from what people think of you to opportunities like jobs and college admissions down the road.

Think about it this way: every tweet you send, every status you update, and every picture you post contributes to a public profile that anyone, including future employers or admissions officers, can see. It's like they have a map of your digital behavior. So, if your online persona is a bit, let's say, wild, it might give them pause. Or, if it's thoughtful and engaging, it could open doors to opportunities you haven't even knocked on yet.

So, how do you ensure your digital footprint is more like a well-tended garden than a wild jungle? Start with a digital audit. Go through your social media profiles with a fine-tooth comb. Look at everything from your posts and pictures to your comments and even your likes. Ask yourself: Does this really represent who I am or who I want to be seen as? If your seventh-grade self thought it was funny to post something a bit edgy, but your ninth-grade self wouldn't dream of it, it might be time for some digital cleanup.

Cleaning up isn't just about deleting a few embarrassing posts. It's about actively protecting your online presence. Remove photos that don't represent your best self, and think twice before sharing that potentially controversial opinion. It's also wise to ramp up your privacy settings. Each social media platform has tools to control who sees what. Dive into those settings and adjust them to protect your info, ensuring only people you trust can see your posts and personal details.

Managing your digital reputation is an ongoing process, not a one-off cleanup job. Regular check-ins on your online presence help keep things in line with who you are and where you're headed. Set a reminder to review your digital footprint monthly. It's like doing regular maintenance on a car—it prevents breakdowns and keeps everything running smoothly.

The future implications of your digital footsteps are significant. Colleges and employers often turn to Google for a snapshot of applicants before making decisions. They're not just looking for red flags like inappropriate content; they're also looking for positives, like your involvement in community projects or your passion for art or coding, showcased through your posts. In a world where your online and offline lives are increasingly blurred, what you share digitally speaks volumes about who you are and what you value.

Navigating the digital world with an awareness of the footprints you leave behind empowers you to build a positive online reputation that opens doors rather than closes them. By conducting regular audits, managing your privacy settings, and being mindful of what you share, you're taking charge of your digital narrative, ensuring it's a true reflection of the awesome person you are becoming. So next time you post, pause and think about the footprints you're leaving in the digital sand. Make each step count, shaping a path to a future you're excited to step into.

4.4 MANAGING SCREEN TIME: FINDING THE RIGHT BALANCE

Hey, ever find yourself glued to your screen, scrolling endlessly, and then wondering where the time went? It happens to the best of us. Screens are like digital candy—super sweet, fun, and easy to overindulge. But just like candy, too much screen time can lead to some not-so-great side effects, like eye strain, sleep troubles, and missing out on some epic real-world adventures. So, how do you strike that perfect balance between tapping and typing and living your life offline? Let's break it down.

First, let's get honest about how much time you spend on those screens. It's like keeping a food diary but for your digital diet. Track your screen time for a few days. You might be surprised to find out just how much time you're spending on apps, games, and browsing. Most smartphones nowadays have built-in tools to help you monitor this, showing you a breakdown of how much time you spend on each app. It's like having a mini-accountant keeping tabs on your digital spending! Seeing the numbers can be a real eye-opener and the first step toward cutting down.

Now, about setting those limits—it's like setting a budget. Decide how much screen time feels reasonable during school days and weekends. Maybe that's an hour on weeknights and a couple more on weekends. Stick to your limits by setting alarms or using apps that remind you when your screen time is up for the day. It's about creating a routine with plenty of time for face-to-face interactions, outdoor activities, and maybe some quiet time to daydream. Remember, the goal here isn't to cut out screens entirely—they're a part of our lives, after all—but to ensure they don't take over.

Speaking of taking over, let's remember the fantastic world of physical activities! Swapping some screen time for some sweat time has loads of benefits. It's not just good for your body; it's a mega boost for your brain too. Regular physical activity can improve your mood, help you sleep better, and sharpen your focus—handy for acing those tests! So, what'll it be? Skateboarding, swimming, dancing, or maybe karate? Find an activity that makes you excited to move. Organize a pick-up basketball game, try out for the school play, or even start a weekend hiking club with friends. Make it fun, make it social, and watch how it transforms not just your body but your whole vibe.

Lastly, let's chat about the perks of dialing down your screen time. Better sleep is a big one. Screens emit a kind of light that can mess with your sleep hormones, making it harder to catch those zzz's. By turning off screens an hour before bed, you're telling your brain it's time to wind down, setting the stage for some sweet dreams. Improved focus is another bonus. Less time flicking through feeds means more time for your brain to dive deep into whatever you're learning or doing. And let's not forget about relationships. More offline time means more opportunities to connect with family and friends in real life. Sharing laughs, trading stories, and making memories—no WiFi necessary.

So, think of managing your screen time as part of taking care of your overall well-being. It's about making room in your day for all kinds of experiences—digital and real-world—and finding that sweet spot where you feel connected, engaged, and balanced. Whether it's through tracking and setting limits, replacing screen time with sweat time, or just enjoying the benefits of unplugging now and then, you're in charge of the remote control of your life. Make sure you're tuning into the proper channels.

4.5 PRIVACY SETTINGS: KEEPING YOUR INFORMATION SAFE

Let's turn our detective skills towards something super crucial in the digital world—your privacy settings. Think of them as the secret passcodes that keep your personal fortress secure from invaders. Just like you wouldn't leave your front door to the house wide open when you go out, you shouldn't leave your digital doors wide open either. Whether it's Facebook, Instagram, Snapchat, or any other platform where you hang out online, each of these spaces has its own set of tools designed to help you control who sees what about you.

Getting to grips with these settings might sound as fun as watching paint dry, but it's less about the chore and more about keeping your digital life as tidy and safe as your bedroom. Each social media platform has its own privacy dashboard, and spending some time there is like doing a security check. You can adjust who can see your posts, who can tag you, and even who can comment on your photos. Facebook, for instance, lets you customize your post visibility right down to specific people.

Instagram offers similar settings, plus the option to make your entire account private, turning it into your personal VIP club.

But here's where it gets tricky—every app updates now and then, and sometimes, these updates can reset your settings without you even noticing. So, it's a good idea to regularly check your settings like you'd check your pockets before heading out. Make it a monthly ritual—like a digital spring cleaning. This keeps you in control, and your private information is just that—private.

Now, let's chat about keeping your personal info under wraps. Some stuff should never make it onto social media—things like your home address, phone number, or daily routine. Sharing these can be like leaving breadcrumbs for trouble to follow. And here's a pro tip: be wary of quizzes and games that ask for personal info. They can be fun, but sometimes they're just a way to fish for your personal details. If you ever accidentally share something sensitive, don't panic. Most platforms have a way for you to delete posts or edit your details. Just dive into your account settings or support pages; they're like the customer service desk for your online life.

Interactive Element: Privacy Check-Up Quiz

Ready to test your privacy savvy? Try this quick quiz to see if you can spot which settings are safe and which might need a rethink.

**Quiz: Digital Privacy Check-up

1. How often do you change your passwords?

    a) I've never changed them.
    b) Once a year.
    c) Every few months.
    d) Whenever I feel it's needed or after a security
        warning.

2. When creating a new password, what do you usually do?

a) Use something easy to remember like my pet's
   name.
b) Use the same password for all my accounts.
c) Use a mix of letters, numbers, and symbols.
d) Let a password manager create a strong password
   for me.

3. What do you do if you receive a friend request or message from someone you don't know online?

a) Accept it—they might be nice!
b) Check their profile and then decide.
c) Ignore it and move on.
d) Block the person and report it.

4. How do you usually connect to Wi-Fi when you're out in public?

a) I connect to any free Wi-Fi available.
b) I use Wi-Fi only if I know the place, like a café or
   school.
c) I avoid public Wi-Fi unless it's secure.
d) I use a VPN (Virtual Private Network) when
   connecting.

5. How do you share personal information, like your phone number or home address, online?

a) I share it with anyone who asks.
b) I share it only with friends in private messages.
c) I never share personal information online.

    d) I double-check and think carefully before sharing
       anything.

6. What's the first thing you do when you receive an email or message with a link from an unknown source?

    a) Click on it to see what it's about.
    b) Ask a friend if they've seen something similar.
    c) Delete it immediately.
    d) Check the sender and hover over the link to see
       where it leads before deciding.

7. How do you manage your social media privacy settings?

    a) I don't really check them.
    b) I leave them on the default settings.
    c) I review and adjust them once in a while.
    d) I regularly check and update my privacy settings
       to limit who can see my posts.

8. What do you do if you see something online that makes you uncomfortable or feel unsafe?

    a) Ignore it and hope it goes away.
    b) Tell a friend but not an adult.
    c) Block or report it immediately.
    d) Talk to a trusted adult about what happened.

See answer key page...

Remember, keeping your digital life secure is just as important as locking up when you leave the house!

Navigating the web safely also means being smart about where you browse. Ever heard of phishing? It's not the kind with rods and reels, but it's definitely trying to catch something—your personal information. Phishing happens when sneaky emails or websites pretend to be legit to trick you into giving up your passwords or other info. Always double-check the URLs of sites you visit (look for that little lock icon next to the web address), and be cautious with emails asking for your details, even if they look real. If something feels off, it probably is; that's your spidey sense.

Let's remember those software updates that pop up at the most annoying times. Yes, they can be a hassle, but they're also essential for patching security holes and protecting your digital walls against intruders. So, next time your device suggests an update, consider it a reinforcement of your online armor and let it do its thing.

So, keeping your digital life secure is a mix of setting strong boundaries, staying sharp about what you share, and keeping your software up to date. Just like in the real world, staying safe online means paying attention to the locks, alarms, and the company you keep. Treat your digital space with the same care and respect as your personal space, and you'll navigate this digital world like the savvy netizen you are!

4.6 VIRTUAL FRIENDSHIPS: KEEPING THEM HEALTHY AND RESPECTFUL

Navigating the world of online friendships can often feel like you're exploring a vast, exciting landscape—you meet new people, share interests, and connect over everything from your favorite video games to the latest viral memes. But just like in the real world, it's super important to cultivate healthy, respectful, and genuine relationships.

So, what does a healthy online friendship look like? It's built on mutual respect, honesty, and setting appropriate boundaries—kind of like having a sturdy fence that ensures everyone's comfort zone is respected. A good virtual friend respects your opinions, even when they differ, and supports you rather than tearing you down. They keep your secrets safe and don't push you to share more than you want. This kind of friendship feels like a two-way street, where both of you benefit and contribute equally, rather than a one-sided highway where one person's needs dominate the traffic.

But hey, not all online interactions are smooth sailing. There are red flags that can signal you're heading into rough waters. If someone constantly demands your attention, disrespects your boundaries, or makes you uncomfortable by oversharing personal info, these are warning signs as glaring as a neon 'STOP' sign. It's crucial to recognize these early on. If you're chatting on social media or a gaming site, and someone starts acting possessive or lashes out when you don't reply immediately, it's time to reassess that friendship. It's like knowing when to hit the brakes before you end up in a friendship fender-bender.

Transitioning online friends to offline buddies is another exciting journey, but it comes with its own set of road rules. Meeting an online friend can be as thrilling as the finale of your favorite series, but safety always comes first. Always choose a public place for your first meetup—think a coffee shop, a popular park, or a local library. These spots are not only safe but also neutral ground, making the meeting less intimidating. And here's a pro tip: bring along a trusted adult or a friend. It's like having a co-pilot who helps you navigate this new experience safely.

Maintaining respect and kindness in your online interactions is non-negotiable. Behind every username and profile picture is a real person with feelings, dreams, and struggles. Always pause and think before you comment or message. Ask yourself, "Would I say this to their face?" If not, it's probably best left unsaid. This approach fosters positive interactions and builds a digital environment where everyone feels valued and safe. It's about putting the 'friend' in 'friendship,' ensuring your digital world is as warm and welcoming as your real one.

Navigating virtual friendships with care enriches your online experiences and builds connections that can last a lifetime. By fostering respect, setting boundaries, and ensuring safety when meeting online friends, you create a network that supports and enhances your digital life. Remember these tips as you continue to connect and grow your circle, and remember, a little kindness goes a long way in the digital world.

As we close this chapter on navigating the complex yet fascinating world of digital interactions, remember the importance of balance, respect, and safety. Each step and strategy we've explored not only enhances your online experiences but also ensures they complement your offline life, creating a harmonious blend of the two. Looking ahead, we'll dive into the exciting world of extracurricular activities in the next chapter, exploring how they can enrich your school experience, expand your skills, and offer fun ways to explore your passions. Get ready to step out of the digital realm and into a world of diverse and enriching activities that await you!

EXTRACURRICULAR AND PERSONAL GROWTH

Welcome to the wild and wonderful world of extracurricular activities! Think of this chapter as your all-access pass to the backstage of the school life concert—beyond the core classes and into the sparkly world of clubs, sports, and arts. It's where the magic of self-discovery happens, where you might find yourself, or at least find out whether you're more of a debate club champ or a chess club wizard. So, let's jump right in and explore how you can pick the perfect extracurricular activities that resonate with your inner superstar!

5.1 FINDING THE RIGHT EXTRACURRICULAR: A GUIDE FOR EVERY INTEREST

First off, let's figure out what floats your boat. It's like being at a huge buffet—you won't know your favorite dish unless you know what's on the menu and your mood. Start by taking a good look at what you enjoy and what you're good at. Maybe you have a knack for making people laugh (future improv star?), or perhaps you find yourself doodling on every surface you can find (hello, future graphic designer!).

To get a clearer picture, ask yourself about your favorite subjects, your hobbies, and how you like to spend your free time. Pondering these questions can reveal surprising truths about your interests and guide you toward activities you might not have considered before. Plus, it's a fun way to learn about yourself without having to write an essay on "Who Am I?" Try this Personality Quiz.

Quiz: What's Your Inner Superhero?

Discover which superhero matches your personality! Answer these questions to find out which amazing powers and traits you have hidden within!

1. What's your favorite way to spend a Saturday?

   a) Hanging out with friends and playing games.
   b) Reading a cool book or learning something new.
   c) Exploring the outdoors and going on adventures.
   d) Helping others or volunteering.

2. Which of these animals do you like the most?

   a) Cheetah – fast and fierce.
   b) Owl – wise and observant.
   c) Dolphin – playful and social.
   d) Dog – loyal and caring.

3. If you had a superpower, what would it be?

   a) Super speed!
   b) Mind reading.
   c) The ability to fly.

d) Healing powers.

4. How do you solve a problem?

a) Quickly and confidently, I jump right in!
b) I think it through carefully before deciding.
c) I ask for advice or work with others.
d) I try to understand everyone's feelings first.

5. What's your favorite subject in school?

a) P.E. or sports – I love being active.
b) Math or science – I like solving puzzles.
c) Art or music – I enjoy being creative.
d) Social studies or history – I'm interested in people
   and the world.

6. Which snack do you prefer?

a) Energy bar or something quick to eat on the go.
b) Fruit or something healthy and brain-boosting.
c) A sandwich or something you can share.
d) Chocolate or something sweet that makes people
   smile.

7. What's your favorite color?

a) Red – bold and bright.
b) Blue – calm and cool.
c) Green – natural and fresh.
d) Yellow – sunny and cheerful.

8. How do your friends describe you?

a) Energetic and fun.
b) Smart and thoughtful.
c) Creative and adventurous.
d) Kind and caring.

See answer key page...

Explore Available Options

Now that you have a better idea of your likes and potential skills let's see what your school or community has to cook up. Schools are often brimming with clubs and teams ranging from sports like soccer and basketball, to the arts like drama and choir, to special interest groups like the robotics club or the environmental club. Each of these is a mini-adventure waiting for you, packed with new learning and new friends.

But don't stop at the school gates! Your community likely has a bunch of activities, too—think local theater groups, dance classes, or even a young volunteers group. These can be great ways to dive deeper into your interests and meet people from different schools, or even different age groups, expanding your social circle and your horizons at the same time.

Consider Time and Commitment

Before you sign up for every club under the sun, let's talk about the nitty-gritty: time management. Every activity sounds great until you realize there are only 24 hours in a day, and you probably should spend a few of them sleeping. Look at how much time each activity requires, and consider how it fits into your current schedule. Does the drama club meet at the same time as the science tutoring you committed to? That's going to be a bit of a pickle.

Be realistic about what you can commit to without turning your school week into a tornado of activities. It's great to be involved, but you'll enjoy it more if you're not rushing from one thing to another, feeling like a juggler with too many balls in the air.

Trial and Error: The Spice of Life

Here's the most important piece of advice: give yourself permission to try and switch. Maybe you joined the basketball team but realized your hand-eye coordination is better suited to video games than free throws. That's totally okay! Think of each activity as a 'trial run'. You're testing out what works for you and what doesn't.

Remember, finding the right extracurricular activity can sometimes be a process of elimination as much as selection. If something doesn't fit, give something else a shot. Maybe swap the basketball for a debate team membership—less running, more arguing (in a structured, educational setting, of course).

Interactive Element: "What's Your Extracurricular Match?"

Curious about which extracurricular might light up your world? Who knows? You might discover a hidden passion for underwater basket weaving or find you're a chess prodigy in the making! Take this quiz to match your interests and personality with potential school clubs and activities.

Extracurricular Activities Quiz

Assess Personal Interests and Skills

Find out which school club or activity is perfect for you! Answer these questions to discover your ideal extracurricular activity.

1. What's your favorite part of the school day?

    a) Hanging out with friends and chatting.
    b) Getting creative in art class.
    c) Solving challenging problems in math or science.
    d) Participating in gym class or playing sports.
    e) Helping others or organizing events.

2. Which hobby do you enjoy the most?

    a) Writing stories, poems, or in a journal.
    b) Drawing, painting, or crafting.
    c) Building things or experimenting with gadgets.
    d) Playing a sport or exercising.
    e) Volunteering, helping out at home, or planning parties.

3. If you could spend a whole weekend doing one activity, what would it be?

    a) Reading a great book or writing a blog.
    b) Creating art, taking photos, or making music.
    c) Coding a game, working on a science project, or fixing something.
    d) Playing sports or going on an adventure.
    e) Organizing a charity event or leading a group activity.

4. How do you usually handle group projects?

a) I like to write and share ideas.
b) I contribute by designing or making things look great.
c) I'm the one who figures out how to solve problems or create solutions.
d) I like to keep everyone motivated and active.
e) I take charge and make sure everything gets done on time.

5. Which of these best describes you?

a) Expressive and communicative.
b) Creative and imaginative.
c) Logical and analytical.
d) Energetic and competitive.
e) Responsible and organized.

6. What's your favorite way to relax after school?

a) Reading, writing, or watching interesting videos.
b) Drawing, painting, or making music.
c) Playing video games, building models, or working on a project.
d) Playing a sport or going for a run.
e) Planning my next big idea or helping out around the house.

7. If you could join a school club right now, what would it be?

a) The school newspaper or writing club.
b) Art club, music club, or drama club.
c) Robotics club, science club, or chess club.
d) Sports team or outdoor adventure club.
e) Student council, community service club, or event
planning committee.

See answer key on page...

Diving into extracurricular activities is one of the best parts of school life. It's your chance to explore, meet like-minded friends, and grow skills you never knew you had. So go ahead, try something new, stick with what you love, and let's make this school year not just about grades but about growing your passions and discovering new ones. Who's ready to explore?

5.2 SPORTS: TEAMWORK AND PERSONAL FITNESS

So, you're thinking about hitting the field, the court, or maybe the track? Sports are more than just a fun way to fill up your after-school hours—they're like your own personal boot camp for body, mind, and social skills. Yeah, you heard that right! Joining a sports team can pump up your fitness level, but it's also great for learning teamwork, building discipline, and boosting your brainpower. Let's lace up our sneakers and dive into how sports can be a game-changer in your school life.

First up, let's talk about the benefits of getting into sports. Imagine your body as a high-powered vehicle—sports can help fine-tune that engine. From increasing your stamina and strength to improving your coordination, regular sports activities keep you in top-notch shape. But the perks don't stop at physical fitness. Ever heard of the 'runner's high'? That's all about endorphins—those feel-good hormones that kick in during physical activity. They're like nature's stress-reliever, helping you feel more relaxed and happy after a game or a vigorous practice session.

But sports aren't just about running around and getting fit. They're also fantastic for your brain. Studies show that students who participate in sports often see improvements in their concentration, determination, and problem-solving skills. It's like each game is a mini-classroom where you learn how to strategize, anticipate your opponent's moves, and make quick decisions. Plus, being part of a team helps you develop awesome social skills. You learn how to communicate under pressure, work cooperatively, and support your teammates, all of which are super important skills both on and off the field.

Now, finding the right sport—that's where you need to play detective a bit. Think about what you enjoy and what you're good at. Do you like fast-paced action? Maybe basketball or soccer is your thing. Prefer something a bit more individual? How about track and field or tennis? And don't forget, sports aren't just about athleticism; they're about passion, too. So, even if you're not the fastest runner or the highest jumper, if you love what you're doing, you're already on the path to success.

It's also wise to think about how a sport fits into your life because let's be honest, there are only so many hours in a day. Understand the commitment you're signing up for—how often are the practices? When are the matches? Make sure it's a schedule you can handle without stressing out or neglecting your homework. After all, you want to be a champ in the classroom as well as in the game.

Speaking of balance, let's not forget about sportsmanship—the real MVP when it comes to playing sports. It's all about playing fair, respecting your opponents, and handling wins and losses gracefully. Winning is awesome, sure, but how you play the game says a lot about who you are. Show respect for the other team and for the rules of the game. And when things don't go your way? Shake it off. Every loss is a lesson, and handling it with dignity is a sign of true character.

So, whether you're scoring goals, making baskets, or just giving your all at practice, remember that sports are about so much more than the final score. They're about building a stronger, smarter, and more resilient you. So go ahead, take the shot, join the team, dive into the deep end—whatever sport you choose, you're setting yourself up for a win in the game of life. And hey, who knows? This could be the beginning of something great. Maybe one day, you'll be the one making the crowd go wild. But for now, enjoy the play, learn from your teammates, and keep chasing those athletic dreams.

5.3 ARTS AND CREATIVITY: EXPRESSING YOURSELF OUTSIDE ACADEMICS

Hey, have you ever wondered why doodling on the side of your notebook feels so good or why belting out your favorite song in the shower leaves you grinning from ear to ear? Well, that's the magic of the arts! Engaging in creative activities isn't just fun; it's like giving your brain a joyride. Let's explore the colorful world of arts and creativity, from painting and music to theater and dance, and discover how you can make these activities a regular part of your life, not just a school elective.

Exploring Different Art Forms

Think of the art world as a giant amusement park. Each ride, whether it's the rollercoaster of drama class or the merry-go-round of choir practice, offers its own unique thrill. And the best part? You get to try as many as you want! You may find yourself mesmerized by the calmness of painting landscapes, or perhaps the adrenaline of performing on stage in a play will be more your speed. The key is to dive into different experiences. Most schools offer a variety of arts programs, and many communities have workshops or classes where you can experiment with more unusual activities like pottery, digital art, or even filmmaking. These are all incredible ways to not only learn new skills but also to express what's going on inside your head and heart. Plus, they're a killer way to make your college applications stand out down the road!

Benefits of Artistic Expression

Now, let's chat about why dabbling in the arts is a smart move. For starters, getting creative does wonders for your brain. It's like exercise but for your imagination. Drawing, playing an instrument, or dancing can improve your problem-solving skills, enhance your ability to focus, and even boost your memory. But the perks don't stop there. Emotionally, arts and crafts are a bit like personal therapy. They provide a safe space to express your feelings and can be incredibly soothing. Ever felt a rush of relief after sketching out a tough day at school or felt a burst of pride when nailing a difficult piano piece? That's your emotional well-being getting a nice boost from your creative efforts.

Finding Art Resources and Communities

So, where do you find these creative outlets? Start at school. Join the art club, audition for the school play, or sign up for the band. Not only will you get to polish your skills, but you'll also meet folks who share your interests. It's like finding your tribe—people who speak the same creative language as you. But don't stop there! Check out what your local community has to offer. Many cities have youth orchestras, art classes at museums, or dance studios that welcome teens. Libraries often host writing workshops, and community centers might offer everything from photography classes to theater groups. These places are not just resource gold-mines but also fantastic spots to make new friends who are just as artsy and unique as you are.

Incorporating Art into Daily Life

Now, how about weaving art into your everyday life? It's easier than you think. Start carrying a sketchbook around. You can doodle in it, jot down lyrics, or paste in some cool photos or fabric swatches you find. It becomes a visual journal of your life. Or keep your instrument out of its case and within easy reach. You're more likely to practice if it's staring at you all day! And why not volunteer for the school decorations committee or help out with the set design for the school play? These are fun ways to keep your creative juices flowing while contributing to school life.

And let's not forget technology. Use apps to create digital art or to produce your own music. These tools can help you experiment with different styles and techniques without needing a whole studio. Plus, sharing your creations on social media or platforms like YouTube can be a great way to get feedback and connect with a broader audience who appreciates your work.

Whether it's through painting, music, theater, or dance, embracing the arts opens up a world of possibilities. It helps you express yourself, boosts your brainpower, and connects you with others. So go ahead, pick up that paintbrush, step onto that stage, or hit those high notes. Let your creativity shine, and watch how it transforms not just your school life but your entire world. Keep exploring, keep creating, and most importantly, keep enjoying every moment of your artistic journey. After all, the world is your canvas; paint it as brightly as you can!

5.4 VOLUNTEERING: GIVING BACK AND GROWING

Imagine you're walking through your neighborhood and see someone struggling to carry a bunch of groceries, and you decide to help them out. How awesome does it feel afterward? Pretty great, right? That's a little taste of what volunteering can bring into your life—a sense of accomplishment and a big, hearty dose of feel-good vibes. But hey, it's not just about feeling good; it's about doing good, too. When you volunteer, you're stepping up to help not just individuals but your whole community. It's like being a superhero, but instead of a cape and superpowers, you're armed with your time, your energy, and your willingness to make a difference.

Now, let's dive into how volunteering can seriously amp up your own life. It's not just about the warm fuzzies you get from helping others—though those are pretty great! Volunteering can actually teach you a boatload of skills. Teamwork, for instance, because most volunteer gigs will have you working alongside others. And problem-solving? Absolutely. Whether it's figuring out how to organize a food drive or how to cheer up residents at a senior center, you're going to be flexing those brain muscles. What's more, all these experiences show you real-world applications of what you might be learning in school, like biology concepts at a community garden or math skills when you help manage donations.

But where do you find these golden opportunities? Start local. Check out what's available in your school, like clubs that focus on community service. Maybe there's a group that cleans up local parks or tutors younger students. Your community centers, religious organizations, and even local chapters of big nonprofits like the Red Cross often have programs designed for young volunteers like you. These places are always on the lookout for enthusiastic helpers, and they might just have the perfect spot for you. And don't forget about events! Festivals, charity runs, and other big gatherings often need a crew of volunteers to make things run smoothly.

Let's not breeze past another huge perk of volunteering—the people you'll meet. These aren't just contacts or casual acquaintances. They're potential mentors, friends, and even future colleagues. Networking might sound like something only adults need to worry about, but hey, building your community network now opens up doors for later. Maybe the coordinator of a volunteer program you rock at will write you a stellar recommendation for a job or college application down the line. See? Every bit of effort you put in can circle back in amazing ways.

Now, about keeping track of all these good deeds—not just for feeling proud but also for practical reasons. Maintaining a record of your volunteer activities is super smart. It's not just about tallying hours; it's about keeping notes on what you did, what skills you used, and what you learned. This can be a gold mine when you're applying for colleges or jobs. Plus, reflecting on your experiences can give you insights into what you enjoy and what you're good at, which can guide your future choices, from your studies to your career.

So, why not jump into volunteering? Whether it's planting trees, helping out at a local library, or organizing a charity event, every action you take builds up your community and builds up you too. Don't know where to start, talk to your youth pastor, camp counselors, teachers for ideas, that work for your interests. It's all about taking what you learn in the classrooms and halls of your school and applying it to the real world. You get to see the impact of your actions firsthand and grow into a person who's not just smart but also kind-hearted and responsible. And honestly, the world could always use more people like that. So go ahead, step up, and start making a difference. Your future self—and your community—will thank you!

5.5 LEADERSHIP ROLES: HOW TO STEP UP IN SCHOOL AND BEYOND

Hey, have you ever watched those movies where an ordinary kid steps up, takes the lead, and ends up doing extraordinary things? Well, guess what? That could be you! Stepping into a leadership role, whether in school, a club, or a community group, isn't just for the naturally outspoken or super confident. It's for anyone who wants to make a difference, including you. So let's chat about how you can snag those leadership spots and really shine.

Identifying Leadership Opportunities

First up, spotting opportunities to lead is like being on a treasure hunt—you need to know where to look. Start with your school. Are there clubs or teams that you are already a part of? Often, these groups need a president, a secretary, or other officers to help organize activities and make decisions. And don't forget about student government—that's like the central hub of school leadership roles. It's where you can really influence school policies and activities. But the opportunities don't end at school gates. Look around your community too. Local youth groups, sports teams, and even volunteer organizations often need young people to step up and lead projects or events.

Think about what excites you most. Do you love the idea of organizing events? Maybe leading the planning committee for the next school dance could be your thing. Or perhaps you're passionate about making your school more eco-friendly. Why not run for a position where you can push those green initiatives? The key is to match your interests with the roles available. That way, you're more likely to enjoy your responsibilities and stick with them.

Developing Leadership Skills

Now, being a leader isn't just about taking charge—it's about inspiring others, making smart decisions, and sometimes, handling tough situations. So, how do you build those skills? Start with communication—it's the golden key in your leadership toolkit. Great leaders know how to express their ideas clearly and listen to others. Practice this in your everyday interactions. Listen actively to your friends, try to really understand their points of view, and share your thoughts without bulldozing over theirs.

Responsibility is another big one. When you're a leader, people count on you to follow through. You can build this skill in small ways, like being on time for meetings or keeping your promises to friends. Start small, and as you get more comfortable, take on bigger tasks. It's like lifting weights—start light and gradually increase as you get stronger.

Motivating others is also crucial. Ever had someone cheer you on so enthusiastically that you felt you could run an extra mile? Be that person for your team. Celebrate small victories, encourage your peers when things get tough, and always keep the mood light and positive. It's about creating an environment where everyone feels valued and motivated to give their best.

Handling Leadership Challenges

Alright, let's be honest—being a leader isn't always a walk in the park. There will be challenges, like dealing with conflicts or making tough decisions. When conflicts arise, stay calm and neutral. Listen to all sides and try to come up with a fair solution. It's like being a referee in a game—you need to see the whole field to make the right call.

Making decisions can be scary, too, because, let's face it, not every decision will please everyone. When you face a tough choice, gather as much information as you can, weigh the options, and think about what's best for the group as a whole. It's not about what's popular; it's about what's right. And remember, it's okay to make mistakes. Every misstep is a chance to learn and grow.

Benefits of Leadership Experience

Stepping into leadership roles can transform you in ways you might not expect. You'll build confidence as you overcome challenges and see your plans in action. You'll also boost your college applications and job resumes—after all, colleges and employers love seeing that you've taken the initiative and held responsible roles.

But beyond the resume boosters, leadership shapes you as a person. It teaches you about integrity, about standing up for what you believe in, and about bringing out the best in others. These are skills that go way beyond school or job applications—they're life skills that will serve you well no matter where you go or what you do.

So why not step up and take on a leadership role? Whether you're guiding a project, leading a club, or representing your classmates, you're gaining experiences that will shape your future. It's about making a difference, growing as a person, and maybe, just maybe, finding out that you're a leader who can inspire change and make things happen. Who knows? This could be the start of something big, and it all begins with that first step forward. So go ahead, take the lead, and see where it takes you!

5.6 HOBBY HUNTING: DISCOVERING NEW PASSIONS

Hey there! Have you ever considered that your after-school fun could be more than just a way to chill out? Yep, we're talking hobbies—the stuff you do for the sheer joy of it, like coding, baking, or even gardening. These aren't just fillers for your free time; they're potential gold mines for skills and maybe even your future career. Let's explore how you can dig into these hobbies and maybe discover new passions that could light up your world.

Exploring new hobbies is like opening a treasure chest—you never know what gems you'll find inside. Beyond the usual school activities, there's a whole universe of hobbies out there waiting for you. Ever thought about coding? It's not just for tech whizzes; it's for anyone who loves solving puzzles. Or maybe you're the next master chef in waiting? Cooking can be more than making a killer grilled cheese sandwich; it's about experimenting with flavors and perhaps even impressing your friends and family with some gourmet dishes.

And here's the thing about hobbies—they don't have to stay in the "just for fun" category. They can actually give you a head start on your future. For example, dabbling in coding doesn't just mean you're killing time; you're building critical thinking and problem-solving skills that are gold dust in almost any career. And cooking? Beyond just being a life skill, it teaches you creativity, timing, and how to handle a crisis (like when that cake decides not to rise).

Now, where do you find the resources to kickstart these potential career-launching hobbies? Your community is a treasure trove of opportunities. Local clubs and online communities abound for almost any interest under the sun. Libraries often host coding workshops, community centers might offer cooking classes, and don't forget about the virtual world. Websites and forums can connect you with experts and enthusiasts in whatever hobby catches your fancy. These platforms aren't just places to learn; they're places to connect and grow your passion into something that might one day define your career.

Integrating these hobbies into your daily life is the key to transforming them from a pastime to a passion. Say you're into photography; why not start a project capturing everyday moments around your school or community? Or if you're into coding, try building an app that solves a problem you care about. Whatever your hobby, the trick is to weave it into your routine until it becomes a part of who you are—not just something you do.

In essence, hobbies are more than escapes from the daily grind of school. They're stepping stones to learning new skills, discovering your passions, and maybe even deciding on a future career path. They enrich your life, giving you tools to develop career skills and opening doors you might not even know existed. So go ahead, pick a hobby or two, and dive deep. Who knows what you'll discover about the world and yourself?

Visual Element: Hobbies and Career Skills Infographic

Check out this cool infographic that connects popular hobbies with the professional skills they build. See how playing video games can enhance strategic thinking, or how painting can boost your creativity and problem-solving skills in real-world scenarios!

Hobbies are more than just fun—they're a playground for personal and academic growth. They challenge you to learn new things, solve problems, and manage your time effectively. They can spark a lifelong passion or even point you toward a future career. So why not explore a new hobby today? Dive into coding, start a sketchbook, join a gardening club, or hit the kitchen and whip up some culinary delights. Each hobby holds the promise of new skills, new challenges, and endless fun. Plus, it's a great way to spice up your college applications and show off your well-rounded self!

As we wrap up this chapter on hobbies and their hidden benefits, remember that these activities are more than just sidelines. They're opportunities for growth, learning, and maybe even finding your calling. So keep exploring, keep enjoying, and who knows? Your hobby today might just turn into your career tomorrow.

REAL STORIES, REAL ADVICE

6.1 OVERCOMING ACADEMIC CHALLENGES: STORIES OF RESILIENCE

Ever felt like school was a giant puzzle, and you were handed the box without the picture on it? You're not alone. Every day, countless students wrestle with academic challenges, from decoding the mysteries of algebra to mastering the magic of essay writing. But here's the kicker—not all battles in the classroom are about getting the right answers. Sometimes, they're about finding new ways to learn and overcoming hurdles that seem as high as Mount Everest. Let's dive into some real-life tales of resilience and the strategies that turned struggles into triumphs.

Imagine this: Emily, a bright-eyed eighth grader, always found math as confusing as trying to read a book upside down. Numbers were mixed up, formulas forgot their places, and percentages were a foreign language. It wasn't just tough; it was discouraging. But here's where Emily's story twists: instead of waving the white flag, she sought help, joining a math tutoring group after school. This wasn't just any group. It was a band of math warriors, each with their own battles and victories. With the guidance of a tutor who was part wizard, part cheerleader, she slowly but surely began to unravel the mysteries of math. The breakthrough came when she realized that formulas were just puzzles waiting to be solved and that she was a puzzle master in the making. Emily's journey wasn't just about improving her grades but transforming her fear of failure into a love for learning.

Let's not forget the person who often sees the struggle before anyone else does—the teacher. Mr. Thompson, a veteran science teacher, had a sixth sense for spotting students in distress. He noticed when Jake, usually enthusiastic about science, began to retreat during lab sessions. His grades slipped like notes under a door. Mr. Thompson reached out, not with lectures, but with genuine concern. He learned that Jake was overwhelmed, juggling school and helping at home. Together, they developed a plan that included study sessions during lunch and connecting Jake with a senior student mentor. Mr. Thompson's insight and timely intervention helped Jake navigate through his stormy school days, reminding us that teachers are often the unsung heroes in our academic stories.

Now, let's sprinkle some magic dust of encouragement. Overcoming academic challenges isn't just about passing tests; it's about learning that perseverance is as important as knowledge. Every time you stumble in school, you're not falling; you're just learning how to get up stronger. It's about developing a growth mindset, the belief that your abilities can improve over time. Like a video game, every level you conquer in school teaches you new skills and prepares you for bigger challenges. And remember, every hero has a story of a battle they almost didn't win, so why should yours be any different?

Interactive Element: Resilience Journal Prompt

To wrap up, why not grab a journal and jot down a time when you faced an academic challenge? What was it, how did you feel, and what strategies helped you overcome it? Reflecting on your own tale of resilience can be your secret weapon for future challenges. Imagine your journal as a treasure chest of experiences, each entry a gem that reminds you of your strength and courage.

In the grand storybook of middle school, chapters of academic challenges are inevitable. But with the right strategies, a supportive cast of characters, and a hefty dose of perseverance, you can turn any tale of struggle into a victory dance. So the next time you face a mountain of homework or a project that seems impossible, remember Emily's puzzle-solving epiphany and Jake's journey with Mr. Thompson and know that you, too, have the power to write your own success story.

6.2 SOCIAL WINS AND WOES: REAL KIDS' EXPERIENCES

Middle school social life is a bit like a live-action role-playing game. Each day, you might take on a different role: the brave knight in a group project, the lone wolf in the cafeteria, or the wise sage offering advice to a friend. And just like any game, there are wins, losses, and lessons to be learned along the way. Let's explore a tapestry of real stories from kids who've navigated the complex social scene of middle school, uncovering the strategies that helped them, the lessons they learned, and the advice they have to share.

Picture this: Lucas, a seventh-grader, had always floated between social circles, never really anchoring himself to any particular group. One day, he found himself at the center of a rumor mill—a place no one wants to be. Misunderstandings over a misconstrued conversation had painted him in an unflattering light. Initially, Lucas felt isolated, like a ship adrift. But instead of letting the rumors define his middle school experience, he took a proactive approach. He reached out directly to his classmates, clearing up the misunderstanding with honesty and a bit of humor. Lucas learned that direct communication could cut through the noise of middle school drama faster than any rumor could spread. From then on, he became a sort of diplomat, helping others resolve misunderstandings before they turned into social wildfires.

Now, meet Ava, a sixth-grader who accidentally stumbled upon her social superpower. Shy by nature, Ava often felt invisible in the bustling hallways of her school. But everything changed during a group project on ancient civilizations. Ava discovered she had a knack for storytelling, transforming dry historical facts into vivid tales that captivated her classmates. This newfound skill won her respect and a circle of friends who appreciated her unique contributions. Ava's story teaches us that sometimes, the things we're passionate about can also be the key to unlocking our social potential. By sharing her love for history, she not only boosted her self-esteem but also connected with peers who shared her interests.

On the flip side, there's the tale of Mia, who found herself on the painful end of a friendship breakup. Best friends since kindergarten, Mia and her friend Zoe had promised they'd navigate middle school together. But as new interests and new friends entered the scene, their paths diverged, leaving Mia feeling abandoned. It was a tough lesson on the sometimes-fluid nature of relationships. Through this experience, Mia learned the importance of diversifying her social portfolio, so to speak. She joined a robotics club, where she not only indulged her love for tech but also formed new friendships that were based on shared passions rather than history. Mia's advice to her peers? Don't put all your emotional eggs in one friendship basket. Expand your horizons, and you might just find a world of friendships you never knew existed.

Each of these stories shines a light on the complex but rewarding world of middle school social life. From Lucas's diplomacy to Ava's storytelling prowess and Mia's resilience in the face of change, these experiences underscore the importance of developing strong social skills. Empathy, communication, and conflict resolution aren't just academic terms; they're real tools that can help you navigate the social maze of middle school. They're your armor and your compass, guiding you through the daily interactions and helping you build relationships that can withstand the tests of time and change.

So, as you step into the bustling social scene of middle school, remember these tales. Think of them as your guideposts, offering you strategies, insights, and peer advice that can help you manage your own social challenges. Whether it's dealing with rumors, finding your unique social niche, or handling the shifting sands of friendships, know that you're not alone in this journey.

Like Lucas, Ava, and Mia, you have the power to shape your social world. With a bit of courage, a dash of strategy, and a healthy dose of empathy, you can turn your middle school social experiences from a bewildering maze into a rewarding adventure.

6.3 PERSONAL GROWTH TALES: FROM AWKWARD TO AWESOME

Middle school is like being handed a blank canvas; every brushstroke of experience adds to the masterpiece that is 'you.' Some kids splash bold colors of confidence from the get-go, while others take time, adding careful layers, until they step back and think, "Wow, did I really create that?" Let's talk about some students who turned their 'awkward' into their 'awesome' through personal growth, exploring new interests, and truly embracing their individual journeys.

Take Sam, for instance. In sixth grade, Sam was the quiet kid in class, always lurking in the background, hoping not to be noticed. He dreaded presentations and would turn tomato-red if a teacher even glanced in his direction during class discussions. But then, something changed. Sam discovered the drama club. At first, it was just a place to hide out during lunch breaks, but as he watched rehearsals, something inside him clicked. The stage became less intimidating and more of a challenge. With a nudge from a supportive drama teacher who saw potential in his shy glances, Sam decided to audition for a minor role. To his surprise, he got it, and with each rehearsal, his confidence grew. By the end of eighth grade, Sam wasn't just participating; he was leading cast warm-ups and helping others conquer their stage fright. His transformation wasn't just about acting; it was about finding a voice he never knew he had.

Then there's Jenna, whose story is a dance of self-discovery through art. Art class was Jenna's refuge, a place where her ideas could spill out without judgment. When a local mural project was announced, Jenna saw her chance. With brushes in hand, she joined a team that would paint a giant wall near the school. The project was massive, way bigger than any canvas she'd tackled. Working alongside students from different grades and backgrounds, Jenna learned about collaboration and leadership. Her concept design was chosen for the mural, a vibrant depiction of community and diversity. This project didn't just brighten a wall; it brightened Jenna's vision of her future. Art was no longer just a hobby; it became her passion and potential career path.

Reflecting on personal growth can be like peering into a kaleidoscope; with each turn, you see new patterns and possibilities. Here's a thought: what moments in middle school will have changed you? Maybe it will be the time you helped organize a school event, discovering a knack for leadership, or the afternoon you spend tutoring a classmate, finding joy in teaching others. These experiences are more than just diary entries; they're stepping stones on your path to personal growth.

Diversity in personal growth stories is as important as diversity in a forest; each unique tree contributes to the ecosystem's richness. Consider your classmates, each embarking on their own growth adventures. Some may find themselves in sports, others in science clubs or volunteering. What's crucial is the celebration of these diverse paths. Embracing each other's differences and supporting each other's growth stories can turn a middle school from just a school into a thriving community where everyone has the space to grow.

In middle school, every day is a new page in your personal growth story. Whether you're stepping onto a stage, wielding a paintbrush, or coding a new app, each experience shapes you. You start middle school as one person, and by the time the final bell rings, you've transformed, ready to paint new canvases and write new chapters. So, keep exploring, keep challenging yourself, and most importantly, keep growing. You are "awesome' and just waiting to be discovered, one brave brushstroke at a time.

6.4 TEACHER'S CORNER: WHAT YOUR TEACHERS WISH YOU KNEW

Ever wondered what's going on behind those glasses perched on your teacher's nose while they scan the room during a test? Or why do they seem to have a sixth sense for when you've maybe, just maybe, not done your homework? Well, strap in because we're about to spill some teacher secrets—not the kind that gets you extra credit, but the kind that might just change how you see the folks standing at the front of the classroom.

First off, teachers wish you knew that learning isn't just about memorizing facts and regurgitating them for a test. It's about understanding how to think critically, solve problems, and apply what you learn in real-world situations. Ever noticed how Mr. Jackson, the science teacher, often asks, "Why do you think that happens?" instead of just telling you the answer? He's not just trying to make your life harder. He's encouraging you to think deeper and connect the dots, which is a skill you'll use way beyond the walls of middle school.

Communication is another biggie. Teachers love it when you talk to them—not just about grades or homework, but about your ideas, concerns, and even your struggles. Got a cool idea for a project? Share it! Confused about a topic discussed in class? Ask about it! Remember, teachers are not mind readers, although they sometimes seem to have that superpower. Open communication can make your school life a whole lot easier. Plus, it shows that you're engaged and proactive, traits that can shine brightly when report card season rolls around.

Now, let's bust some myths. Many students think teachers are just out to catch them in a mistake or that a strict teacher is a mean one. Here's the real scoop: teachers push you because they believe in your potential. When Mrs. Alvarez piles on the homework, it's not because she thinks you don't have enough to do; it's because she's preparing you for the challenges ahead. And strict teachers? Often, they're the ones who care the most. They set high standards not to see you fail, but to help you reach heights you might not even see for yourself yet.

Lastly, teachers wish students understood the effort that goes into teaching. Planning lessons, grading assignments, and managing a classroom full of diverse learners—it's no walk in the park. When you show appreciation, whether it's a simple thank you after class or participating actively during the lesson, it means more than you might think. It turns teaching from a job into a joy. So next time you think about skipping an assignment or zoning out during a lecture, remember that your engagement can light up your teacher's day!

So, the next time you sit down in class, try seeing the day through your teacher's eyes. Understanding these insights can transform your experience in school, turning everyday lessons into exciting opportunities to grow, communicate, and maybe even teach your teacher a thing or two about the wild, wonderful world of being a middle school student. Keep the lines of communication open, challenge yourself to see the reasons behind the rules, and don't forget a little appreciation goes a long way. Who knows? You might just find a new perspective on learning, one that makes school a lot more exciting and a lot less mysterious.

6.5 PARENT PERSPECTIVES: UNDERSTANDING YOUR FAMILY'S ROLE

Navigating middle school is kind of like learning to ride a bike—sometimes you pedal smoothly, and other times, well, it's all wobbly wheels and unexpected tumbles. And just like any good bike-riding lesson, having someone there to help balance the bike and encourage you can make all the difference. That's where parents come in, playing a crucial role in your middle school adventure. Let's roll into some real stories from parents who've been sideline coaches, cheerleaders, and sometimes, emergency mechanics for their middle schoolers.

Take Clara's mom, for instance. Clara was a whirlwind of energy, always bouncing from one activity to another: soccer practice, piano lessons, and a science club. It was like her calendar was on a caffeine buzz! Her mom, seeing Clara stretched thinner than a pizza dough, stepped in not by pulling the brakes but by gently helping Clara prioritize her activities. Together, they figured out which activities made Clara light up (science club and piano) and which ones could be saved for later (soccer). This wasn't about cutting down her interests but about balancing them so Clara could enjoy and excel without burning out. Her mom's proactive approach in discussing and respecting Clara's interests helped her manage her commitments without feeling overwhelmed.

Then there's the story of Ethan's dad, a quiet man who had a knack for turning every car ride from school into a mini heart-to-heart session. While struggling with some tough math content, Ethan felt too embarrassed to speak up in class or ask his friends for help. His dad noticed Ethan's frustration during these drives and started a series of casual chats, just father and son, no pressure. Over time, these talks became a safe space for Ethan to voice his concerns. His dad listened—really listened—and together, they found an online tutor who specialized in turning math woes into math 'Wow's. This simple act of open, supportive dialogue helped Ethan not only improve his math skills but also boosted his confidence in asking for help when he needed it.

Balancing expectations is something all parents juggle. They want to push you to reach your potential but also recognize when to pull back and let you fly at your own pace. Like Maya's parents, who were both engineers and naturally thrilled when Maya showed a flicker of interest in a robotics workshop. Their excitement, however, started morphing into pressure when they began setting goals for her and planning her path to becoming an engineer. It took a heartfelt conversation, where Maya expressed her growing interest in graphic design, for her parents to realize they were drafting her future based on their blueprints, not hers. They dialed back, redirected their support to her chosen interest, and helped her find a graphic design course. This shift wasn't easy, but it was essential in allowing Maya to explore and excel in what truly engaged her, fostering a supportive rather than prescriptive family dynamic.

Engaging more deeply in your school life doesn't mean your parents have to hover like helicopter pilots. It's about them being present in a way that feels supportive, not suffocating. Take Zoe's family, for instance. They made it a point to attend school events, not just the big, flashy ones but also the regular days when students could showcase their projects or share what they'd learned in class. This kind of involvement showed Zoe that her family cared about her school life, boosting her motivation and pride in her schoolwork. It wasn't about checking a box; it was about connecting with her world.

In the grand scheme of things, parents play a multifaceted role in your middle school years. They're there to guide, support, and sometimes just listen. The stories shared here underline the importance of communication, understanding, and mutual respect in the parent-child relationship during these transformative years. As you navigate your own middle school path, remember that it's okay to seek their advice, share your victories and defeats, and even negotiate your independence as you grow. After all, even when you're ready to ride solo, it's always nice to know someone's there, ready to catch you if you fall.

6.6 OLDER STUDENTS' ADVICE: LOOKING BACK AND MOVING FORWARD

Picture this: you're about to step into high school, and it feels like you're standing at the edge of a giant diving board, looking down into an exciting, but kinda scary, pool of opportunities and challenges. Who better to throw you a few swimming tips than those who've just climbed out of the pool, dripping with experiences and insights? Yes, I'm talking about the high schoolers who were in your shoes not so long ago. They've got the lowdown on what they wish they'd known before making the leap, and they're here to share it with you.

Take Marcus, for instance. He's a freshly minted high school sophomore who still remembers the jittery feeling of his first day. His advice? Get organized and stay ahead of your assignments from day one. Middle school might have felt like a breezy bike ride at times, but high school can turn into a mountain biking adventure really fast, with all the ups, downs, and unexpected bumps. Marcus learned the hard way that procrastination is like a flat tire—it won't get you very far. He suggests setting up a solid system for tracking assignments and deadlines as soon as you get your syllabus. Think of it as your GPS through the winding roads of high school academia.

Then there's Emma, a junior who has become something of a social butterfly in high school but had her share of social stumbles back in middle school. Her secret? She learned to branch out and make friends from different circles, discovering that high school is a tapestry of diverse groups, not just a single clique you have to fit into. Emma encourages you to chat with someone new in class, join clubs that pique your interest, and attend school events. It's all about planting seeds in various gardens—you never know which will bloom into amazing friendships.

Navigating the pitfalls of middle school is something both Marcus and Emma wish they'd mastered earlier. Common traps like spreading yourself too thin with too many activities or neglecting to ask for help when subjects get tough can trip you up. They've seen many friends struggle because they didn't balance their commitments or were too shy to ask a teacher for clarification on a tricky topic. Their advice? Keep your schedule balanced like a good diet—mix in academics, extracurriculars, and social time. And never hesitate to raise your hand, either literally in class or metaphorically, by emailing a teacher. It shows you're proactive, not clueless.

Looking ahead is something both high schoolers emphasize. Setting goals for your high school years and beyond can turn a daunting future into a series of achievable steps. Whether it's aiming for a spot on the student council, targeting a GPA for college scholarships, or exploring interests that could turn into a career, having clear objectives keeps you focused. Marcus and Emma suggest sitting down at the start of each school year to map out your goals, adjust as needed, and celebrate the milestones you reach. It's like setting waypoints on your favorite video game— each one you hit brings you closer to the ultimate prize.

As you gear up to make the jump from middle school to high school, remember, it's about more than just surviving; it's about thriving. Take these pearls of wisdom from those who have swam through the high school waters and use them to help navigate your own journey. Organize, socialize, balance, and goal-set your way through, and you'll not only make a splash, but you might just enjoy the swim too.

As we close this chapter and look forward to the next, remember that each piece of advice, each story of resilience, and every strategy shared here is a stepping stone to not just surviving but thriving through your school years. These insights form a mosaic of experiences, each highlighting a path trodden by those ahead of you. So take heart, plan well, and dive into the next chapter of your life with confidence and curiosity. Onward to the next adventure!

BUILDING RESILIENCE AND POSITIVE MINDSETS

Imagine middle school as a giant, twisty roller coaster—sometimes you're screaming for joy, and other times you're just screaming. But what if I told you that you could be one of those cool kids who keeps their hands up during the whole ride, enjoying each dizzying loop and turn? That's what building resilience is all about. It's your secret ticket to not only surviving the ride but actually waving your hands in the air like you just don't care. So, buckle up; we're about to take off into the world of bouncing back better than ever!

7.1 CULTIVATING RESILIENCE: TECHNIQUES FOR BOUNCING BACK

Understanding Resilience

First off, let's get our heads around what resilience really means. Picture this: You're building a tower out of blocks. Every now and then, someone bumps the table, and blocks fall off. Annoying, right? But resilience is your ability to start stacking those blocks again, maybe even finding a way to strengthen the base. It's about bouncing back from setbacks, whether it's a bad grade, a fight with a friend, or a missed goal in soccer, and not letting it knock you down for long.

Resilience-Building Activities

Now, building resilience sounds great, but how do you actually do it? It's like building muscle—you need the right exercises. So, let's pump up your resilience workout. Start by setting personal challenges that push you a little out of your comfort zone. Maybe that's trying out for the school play, joining a new club, or speaking up more in class. Each challenge you take on builds your confidence and shows you that you can handle more than you think.

Problem-solving tasks are another great tool. The next time you hit a snag—like forgetting your homework or dealing with a canceled plan—instead of freaking out, take a deep breath and start brainstorming solutions. Could you email your teacher? Could you reschedule your plan? Viewing problems as puzzles to solve, not disasters keeps your mind focused on finding solutions, which is crucial to being resilient.

And remember the power of team sports or group activities. Whether it's soccer, drama club, or a science team, working with others towards a common goal can teach you loads about handling ups and downs. Plus, the support and camaraderie of a team is like having a safety net, making sure that if you fall, you're bouncing right back up.

Learning from Setbacks

Remember our block tower? Every time it tumbles, you learn something new about balance and structure. It's the same with life's setbacks. Every mistake, every hiccup, has something to teach you. So, next time something goes wrong, instead of beating yourself up, ask yourself: What can I learn from this? Maybe you'll see that you need to manage your time better or that you need to communicate more clearly. Turning setbacks into learning moments changes them from something negative to something incredibly valuable.

Support Networks

Let's talk about your squad—the people who cheer you on, pick you up and stand by you through thick and thin. Having strong support networks, including family, friends, and mentors, is like having a lifeboat that keeps you floating even when the sea gets rough. These are the people who will remind you of your strengths when you forget, offer advice when you're stuck, and give you a pep talk when you're down. Keep these connections strong by being there for them, too; resilience is a team sport, after all.

Interactive Element: Resilience Journal

To wrap up this resilience rally, why not start a resilience list? Each day, jot down or draw a picture of something challenging you faced and how you dealt with it or a setback you learned from. Over time, you'll have a personal playlist that shows just how much you've grown and all the hurdles you've overcome. Plus, it's a great reminder that no matter what comes your way, you have the skills and the support to handle it.

So, as you roll along this wild ride of middle school, remember: resilience isn't about never falling—it's about how quickly and strongly you can bounce back. And with these strategies in your back pocket, you're ready to keep your hands up and enjoy the ride, knowing that you're equipped to handle every twist and turn. Here's to building resilience and making those middle school years not just survivable but truly spectacular!

7.2 POSITIVE THINKING: REFRAMING YOUR MINDSET

Have you ever had one of those days where everything seems to go wrong, and your brain just keeps replaying the worst moments like a bad movie marathon? Maybe you tripped in the hallway, forgot your homework, or got a lower grade than you expected on a test. It's super easy to let these moments spiral into a storm of negative thoughts. But what if you could switch up the channel and turn those thoughts into something more like a superhero movie, where every challenge is just a step towards saving the day? That's what reframing your mindset is all about!

Let's start with identifying those sneaky negative thought patterns. Catastrophizing is when you blow things out of proportion, like thinking a bad grade means you'll never succeed in anything. Overgeneralizing is another trickster, making you believe that if something bad happens once, it'll happen every time, like assuming you'll always freeze up during presentations just because it happened once. Recognizing these patterns is like being a detective on the lookout for clues of negativity in your mind. Once you spot them, you can tackle them head-on.

Reframing these thoughts means changing that sound of doom into a cheer. For instance, instead of thinking, "I totally bombed that test; I'm so bad at math," try, "Okay, that test didn't go as planned, but I can review what I missed and do better next time." It's like editing your own thought script, where you turn a potential disaster movie into a comeback story. To practice this, next time a negative thought pops up, pause and think of two positive spins you can put on the situation. This exercise isn't just about being optimistic; it's about seeing things in a more balanced, realistic way.

Now, onto the superpowers of positivity. Did you know that keeping a positive mindset can actually boost your brainpower? It's true! When you're positive, your brain is less stressed and more open to tackling tricky problems, whether figuring out a complex math problem or navigating a tough conversation with a friend. Positivity also unlocks creativity, making it easier to come up with out-of-the-box ideas for your projects or finding new ways to organize your study time. It's like giving your brain a pep talk, and who doesn't perform better after one of those?

"What you believe is what will be—So be positive!"

So, how do you keep this sunny outlook shining even on cloudy days? Start each day with a positive affirmation. These are like little banners you hang in your mind that say things like, "I am capable of great things" or "Today is going to be awesome." Say them out loud while you're brushing your teeth, or write them in your journal. And at night, before you sleep, reflect on what went well that day. Maybe you helped a friend, aced a quiz, or just enjoyed a killer lunch. This reflection isn't just about feeling good; it's about training your brain to spot the positives, making it a habit that sticks.

Maintaining a positive outlook might sound like a chore, but think of it more like a game, where each positive thought scores points against the negativity. The more you play, the better you get, and soon, you'll be handling the ups and downs of middle school with the prowess of a seasoned gamer. Remember, every hero has their challenges, but it's their attitude that makes them epic. So, gear up with positivity, reframe those tricky thoughts, and get ready to level up your middle school experience!

7.3 HANDLING FAILURE: LESSONS IN MOVING FORWARD

So, let's talk about a word that makes everyone cringe a little: failure. It's like that one burnt cookie in the batch—you didn't want it to happen, and it's super annoying when it does. But here's a little secret: that burnt cookie, and yes, those moments of failure, have a lot to teach us. In fact, some of the most amazing people you've heard of had their fair share of burnt cookies before they made the perfect batch. Take Michael Jordan, for instance. He was cut from his high school basketball team, but instead of calling it quits, he used that rejection as fuel to work harder, eventually becoming one of the greatest athletes of all time. Or what about Thomas Edison? He didn't invent the perfect light bulb on his first try; it took him thousands of attempts to get it right. Each failure was a lesson, not a stop sign.

Embracing failure as a natural part of learning and growing helps take some of the sting out of it. It's not the opposite of success; it's a step on the path to success. When you start seeing failure this way, it becomes less daunting to step out of your comfort zone and try new things, whether auditioning for the school play, trying out for a new sport, or tackling a challenging class.

Now, when failure does happen—and it will—it's crucial to handle it constructively. Instead of beating yourself up, look for the lesson. Did something not work out the way you planned? Take on the role of a detective and figure out why. Maybe you need to manage your time better, or perhaps you need a new strategy for studying. Once you've pinpointed what went wrong, make a plan for what to do differently next time. This might mean setting aside more time for practice, asking for help, or finding more resources. The key is to turn each 'oops' into a 'let's try that again.'

Building perseverance is like leveling up in a game. The more challenges you face, the stronger you get. One way to build this muscle is to stick with a new skill or hobby, even if it's tough at the start. Remember learning to ride a bike? Those inevitable tumbles didn't stop you from getting back on and trying again. Apply that same grit to learning a new language, playing an instrument, or anything else that doesn't come easy. The satisfaction of finally getting it right after all those attempts is sweet—and it's a great reminder that persistence pays off.

Handling the emotional rollercoaster that comes with setbacks is just as important. Feelings of disappointment, frustration, or even embarrassment are totally normal, but they don't have to derail you. One of the best things you can do is talk about it. Opening up to someone you trust, whether it's a friend, family member, or teacher, can lighten your emotional load and help you gain perspective. Another great tool is writing it out. Writing down your feelings can help clear your mind and allow new ideas and solutions to emerge.

So, as you face various challenges and setbacks, remember that each one holds valuable lessons. By learning to handle failure with grace and determination, seeking feedback, and tapping into your support network, you're not just getting through tough times but growing stronger and more resilient. And who knows? The next time you face a setback, you might just surprise yourself with how well you handle it, turning what could have been a burnt cookie into a chance to tweak the recipe and try again.

7.4 CELEBRATING SUCCESSES: BIG AND SMALL

Imagine your life as one massive highlight reel—every cool project you've nailed, every test you've aced, and even those small wins, like finally nailing the perfect grilled cheese sandwich. These moments, big and small, are like gold stars plastered across your day-to-day life, and guess what? They deserve a celebration. Why? Because recognizing and celebrating your achievements isn't just about giving yourself a pat on the back; it's about fueling your journey forward with confidence and a sense of accomplishment.

Now, let's talk about setting goals. But not just any goals—measurable goals. These are the kind that you can clearly mark as 'done' on your list. Say you want to improve your writing skills. Instead of a fuzzy goal like "get better at writing," how about "write one new short story every month"? This way, you know exactly what you're aiming for, and each completed story is a clear win. It's like setting up checkpoints in a video game; reaching each one gives you a mini celebration moment before you race off to the next level.

But how do you spot these wins, especially the smaller ones that might slip by unnoticed? It starts with paying attention. Maybe you've kept your locker organized for a whole week, or you participated in class more than usual. These achievements might seem small, but they add to big improvements over time. Each one is a step forward in your skills and confidence, and they all deserve a high-five. To make this fun, you could keep a victory log in your planner or on your phone, jotting down all the wins of the week. Then, take a few minutes every Friday to review and celebrate these successes. It's like being the star of your own weekly victory party.

Sharing your successes with others can also magnify the joy. Ever noticed how a smile feels bigger when others smile back? It's the same with sharing your achievements. Whether it's with family, friends, or even a post on your school's online forum, letting others in on your successes opens up a wave of support and celebration that can boost your spirits even higher. Plus, your wins might just inspire your peers to chase their own goals, sparking a cycle of positivity and motivation around you. It's like setting off a firework of good vibes that lights up your whole community.

Now, let's get a bit reflective. Ever thought about how much you've grown over the past year? Keeping a success journal or creating a visual timeline of your achievements can be an eye-opening experience. You could use a notebook, a digital app, or even a series of photos to document your successes. This isn't just about keeping a record; it's about visualizing your growth. Seeing your progress laid out before you can be incredibly inspiring, and it's a concrete reminder that, yes, you are moving forward, even if it doesn't always feel that way.

In this hustle of school life, where tests, projects, and extracurriculars clamor for your attention, taking time to celebrate your successes—big and small—is crucial. It's not just about adding a splash of fun to your routine; it's about recognizing your efforts and reinforcing your path to personal growth. Each celebration is a building block in your self-esteem, each acknowledgment a step toward seeing yourself as the achiever you are. So, go ahead, give yourself that high-five, share your wins, and reflect on how far you've come. After all, every success, no matter the size, is a piece of the awesome puzzle that is you.

7.5 GRATITUDE PRACTICES: ENHANCING YOUR DAILY LIFE

Gratitude is like a superpower that doesn't get enough credit. Imagine it as a magic ingredient that can transform ordinary days into Thanksgiving feasts (minus the turkey and the awkward family conversations). But seriously, practicing gratitude isn't just about saying thanks; it's about changing how you see and interact with the world around you. Focusing on the good stuff—like acing a test, having a good laugh with friends, or simply enjoying a sunny day—amplifies the positive vibes. It can even lead to better sleep, improved mood, and stronger relationships. It's like turning up the brightness on your life's screen.

Now, let's get practical with gratitude journaling. Think of a gratitude journal as your personal highlight reel. Each day, jot down three things you're thankful for. And here's the catch: try not to repeat entries. One day, you might be grateful for your dog's goofy smiles; another day, you might appreciate a really good burger. This practice not only helps you find joy in small moments but also trains your brain to start looking for the positive. It's like setting up a mental filter that catches the good stuff and lets the not-so-great stuff drift by. Plus, on tough days, flipping through your gratitude journal is a quick way to lift your spirits and remind you of the good in your life.

Expressing gratitude to others is another game-changer. Ever told your teacher how much you appreciated their help on a project? Or thanked your friend for always being there to hear you rant? Expressing gratitude can strengthen your relationships and spread some serious joy. It makes the other person feel valued and shows them that you don't take their kindness for granted. So, next time you feel thankful for someone, tell them! It could be as simple as a text, a note, or just a few words when you see them. Watch their face light up—it's pretty much guaranteed.

And here's something you can weave into your daily routine without much fuss: mindful gratitude exercises. Each day, try to find a moment to pause and appreciate something around you. Maybe it's how the morning light filters through your window, the taste of your favorite cereal, or the feeling of a new book in your hands. This practice of noticing and appreciating the little things can make a typical day feel a bit more special. It's like adding a pinch of spice to a dish—it just makes everything better.

Gratitude isn't just for the big wins or happy days; it's a tool that can transform your everyday experience, making life a bit brighter and your interactions a bit sweeter. Plus, it's contagious. Start spreading gratitude, and watch it boomerang right back to you. So, go on, give it a try. What are you grateful for today?

7.6 MINDFULNESS FOR MIDDLE SCHOOLERS: STAYING PRESENT

Ever felt like your mind is a browser with a million tabs open? Homework here, drama there, plus a mental replay of that weird thing you said in class—yikes, it's no wonder you're feeling frazzled. Enter mindfulness, your brain's personal pause button. It's a way to clear out the mental clutter and focus on what's happening right here, right now. Mindfulness might sound a bit out there, but it's actually pretty simple and super useful, especially when it comes to dialing down stress and boosting your focus and mood.

So, what exactly is this simple practice? Mindfulness is all about paying attention to the present moment without any judgment. It's like tuning into your favorite song and really listening to each note and lyric instead of just letting it play in the background while you do a zillion other things. This might sound easy, but when you try it, you'll realize just how often your mind likes to time travel to the past and future. Training it to stay put in the present can be a pretty neat trick for your well-being.

Let's kick things off with some simple mindfulness exercises that you can do anytime, anywhere. First up, focused breathing. This is the backbone of all mindfulness practices. Just sit comfortably, close your eyes, and start to notice your breath. Breathe in deeply through your nose, feel your chest and belly rise, and then slowly breathe out through your mouth. Do this a few times and watch how it helps mellow out your mind and body. It's like hitting the reset button when your computer's acting glitchy.

Next, why not try mindful eating? This isn't about munching on salads all day; it's about really paying attention to what you're eating. Next time you have a snack, take a moment to look at it, smell it, and then eat it slowly, noticing the textures and flavors. It turns a simple snack into a mini adventure for your senses and helps you enjoy the grub more while teaching you to slow down and savor the moment.

Now, have you ever thought about taking a sensory walk? This can be a game-changer. Next time you're walking to school or just around your neighborhood, tune into your senses. What do you see? Maybe the bright colors of the cars, the rusty mailbox at the corner, or the goofy dog wagging its tail. What do you hear? Birds chirping, cars honking? What can you smell? Maybe someone's grilling something yummy. This practice isn't just fun; it helps you connect with the world around you in a refreshingly detailed way.

Incorporating mindfulness into your schoolwork can also work wonders. Before you dive into homework or a big test, take a few minutes to do a mindfulness exercise. This can help clear your mind, reduce anxiety, and boost your concentration. It's like prepping your brain for a workout so it performs better when it's go-time. Whether you're about to tackle algebra problems or write an essay, a little mindfulness beforehand can set you up for success.

Creating a personal mindfulness routine might sound a bit daunting, but it's actually pretty straightforward. Start small; maybe incorporate a minute of focused breathing each morning when you wake up or each night before you go to bed. Then, gradually add more as you get comfortable. The key is consistency. The more regularly you practice mindfulness, the more natural it will feel and the bigger benefits you'll see. It's like leveling up in a game —the more you play, the better you get.

Mindfulness isn't just a one-off tool; it's a super skill that can help you navigate the ups and downs of middle school with a bit more ease and a lot less stress. By staying present, you're not just surviving the school day; you're setting yourself up to thrive in it. So, why not give it a shot? Clear some headspace, tune into the now, and watch how this ancient practice can do some modern magic for your mind and mood.

As we wrap up this exploration of mindfulness, remember that it's all about small, consistent practices that can make a big difference. Whether you're breathing deeply, eating mindfully, or just noticing the world around you, each moment of mindfulness adds up to a clearer, calmer, and more focused you. Now, ready to flip the page? Let's dive into the next chapter, where we'll discover even more ways to make your middle school experience awesome!

PREPARING FOR THE FUTURE

Imagine stepping into a new video game level—new landscapes, tougher challenges, and even cooler power-ups. That's what moving from middle school to high school feels like. It's a whole new adventure, and while it might seem a bit daunting, it's also packed with opportunities to level up in real life. So, let's grab our gear and check out what this new level has in store for us!

8.1 HIGH SCHOOL PREP: WHAT TO EXPECT

Understanding High School Culture

High school isn't just a bigger building with more students; it's a whole new culture. Think of it as upgrading from your cozy community pond to a vast ocean full of diverse creatures and currents. High school students often enjoy more freedom, like choosing electives that match their interests or managing free periods. Plus, there's a wider array of clubs and activities, from robotics teams to poetry slams.

Remember how, in middle school, everyone knew everyone, and news traveled fast? In high school, social circles can be wider and more varied. You might find yourself navigating a social ecosystem that's more complex than a season finale of your favorite series. It's like walking into a party where there are several rooms, each playing different music, and you need to decide where you vibe best. And here's a pro tip: high school is the perfect time to explore different groups and redefine yourself. Ever wanted to unleash your inner poet or debate champ? Now's your chance!

Academic Expectations

Brace yourself—academics in high school can feel like a jump from the kiddie pool to the Olympic-sized one. Classes often dive deeper into subjects, pushing you to think critically and manage your time effectively. For instance, while middle school might have touched on basic biology, high school biology could have you dissecting frogs or exploring complex ecosystems.

Choosing the right subjects becomes crucial because, believe it or not, these choices can influence your future. It's like selecting your character and abilities at the start of a game—choose wisely based on what you love and might want to pursue later. If you're a math wizard, advanced algebra might be up your alley. Got a flair for the dramatic? Theater arts could be your spotlight. And remember, it's totally fine to try a mix early on to see what clicks. High school is as much about discovering your passions as it is about scoring grades.

Extracurricular Opportunities

Here's where high school really starts to sparkle—extracurriculars! These aren't just fillers for your college applications; they are your golden tickets to new skills, friendships, and adventures. High schools often offer a broader range of activities than middle schools. Whether you're into coding drones, writing for the school newspaper, or advocating for environmental issues, there's likely a club or a team for that.

Jumping into these activities can be thrilling. Not only do you get to do more of what you love, but you also meet folks who share your passions. It's like finding your tribe—people who geek out over the same things you do, whether that's debating political issues or crafting the perfect stage set for the school play.

Social Adjustments

Adjusting to the social scene in high school is like learning a new dance. You might stumble a bit at first—figuring out where you fit in the larger, more diverse crowd can take some trial and error. And let's not forget about the age range—you'll be mingling with kids from all grades, which means the freshmen are often the newbies on the block.

Navigating this expanded social landscape means keeping an open mind and maybe even stepping out of your comfort zone. Strike up conversations in the cafeteria, join study groups, or get involved in community service projects. Every interaction is a chance to build new bridges and perhaps discover sides of yourself you didn't know existed.

So, as you gear up for this next phase, think of high school as less of a scary unknown and more of an exciting chapter waiting to be written. It's a place to grow, learn, and transform into whoever you want. With each class, each friend, and each challenge, you're adding lines to your own storylines that tell of triumphs, lessons, and moments of unexpected joy.

8.2 CAREER EXPLORATION: THINKING AHEAD

So, let's chat about something that might seem a bit far off but is actually super important—career planning. I know, I know, you're just in middle school, and it might feel like your career is something you'll think about way in the future, like when you're an actual adult. But trust me, starting to think about it now can be like finding a secret cheat code that makes future levels of the game a whole lot easier. Career planning isn't about deciding right this second what you want to be when you grow up; it's more about exploring what you like, what you're good at and seeing how those things can connect to the world of work.

First up, let's dive into exploring your interests and strengths. This isn't just about figuring out your favorite subjects in school—though that's a great start. It's about discovering what activities make you feel excited, curious, or satisfied. Do puzzles or complex games keep you hooked for hours? Maybe problem-solving or engineering could be your thing. Can you spend all day drawing or crafting? Hello, future in design or arts! To help you along, there are tons of career assessment tools and quizzes online that can be super fun to do. They ask you questions about what you like and don't like, and then they suggest careers that might match your interests and skills. It's like a matchmaking service but for your future job!

Now, let's talk about something really cool—informational interviews and job shadowing. Imagine if you could test-drive a career before deciding if it's right for you. That's pretty much what these are. An informational interview is where you chat with someone who's working in a field you're curious about. You can ask them what their day is like, what they love about their job, and even what they wish they'd known when they were your age. Job shadowing takes it a step further—you actually spend a day or a few hours following someone around at their job. It's like being a detective on a mission to uncover what a day in the life of a graphic designer, scientist, or business manager really looks like.

Setting these up might sound a bit daunting, but it's actually pretty straightforward. Start by thinking of family, friends, relatives, or even teachers who might have careers that interest you. Your school might also help set up these opportunities, so it's worth a chat with your counselor. When you reach out to someone for an interview or shadowing, be polite, tell them you're exploring careers, and ask if they'd be willing to let you learn from them. Most people love talking about what they do and will be flattered to be asked!

Lastly, don't overlook the power of internships and volunteer work. These experiences are gold mines for career exploration. Not only do you get to try out a field, but you also build skills that are great for your resume later on. Plus, you make connections with professionals who can give you advice and might even help you land a job in the future. Whether it's helping out at a local animal shelter, interning at a tech startup, or volunteering at a community center, each experience gives you a taste of different career paths. And hey, the more you try, the clearer your future direction might become.

So, why wait? Dive into discovering what makes you tick, chat with people who are doing awesome things, and try your hand at real-world tasks. It's all about gathering clues that will help you solve the big puzzle of what to do with your life. And remember, it's totally fine if your interests change over time. The goal right now isn't to choose a career but to start understanding the possibilities. Who knows? The perfect job for you might be something you haven't even heard of yet! So stay curious, keep exploring, and enjoy every step of this exciting process.

8.3 DEVELOPING LEADERSHIP SKILLS FOR THE FUTURE

Hey, have you ever thought of yourself as a leader? Maybe the idea sounds a bit massive, like wearing a superhero cape or running a country. But guess what? Leadership isn't just for the chosen few; it's for anyone who decides to step up, and that could totally be you. High school and beyond are packed with chances to take the lead, from student government to debate teams and even leading a volunteer project. Each spot gives you a stage to practice being the kind of leader you'd admire—someone who's fair, makes cool things happen and stands up for others.

So, what does it take to be a good leader? Well, it's not just about being loud or always having the best ideas. Effective leadership is like being the conductor of a band—you help everyone work together to make awesome music. Essential skills include decision-making, weighing the pros and cons, and making choices that benefit the group. Then there's ethical leadership, which is all about doing the right thing, even when it's tough, like admitting a mistake instead of blaming someone else. Conflict resolution is another biggie. Imagine two friends in your group disagreeing. A good leader helps them find common ground instead of letting the argument split the team. And let's not forget public speaking—yep, that means getting comfy with talking in front of others, whether it's at a team meeting or in front of the whole school.

Now, let's bring in some real-life examples to kick things up a notch. Picture Maya, a high school sophomore who noticed that her school's cafeteria was wasting a ton of food. Not cool, right? So, she led a team to start a composting program, teaching everyone how to separate waste and explaining why it mattered. Sure, she faced challenges like getting people on board and sorting out the logistics, but by keeping her cool and showing how composting could help their school garden, she got everyone hyped to join in. Or take Alex, who used his love for video games to create a gaming club at school that not only played games but also raised money for local charities through tournaments. He had to navigate scheduling conflicts and motivate club members, but his clear communication and infectious enthusiasm kept the club thriving.

Feeling inspired? Let's channel that energy into creating your own leadership development plan. This isn't about setting giant, overwhelming goals. Start small. Think about what leadership role you might want to try out next year. You could run for a student council position or lead a project in one of your clubs. Set specific goals, like improving your public speaking by joining the debate club or learning to resolve conflicts by helping to mediate issues during group projects.

Remember, every leader started somewhere and didn't always get it right the first time. Leadership is a journey—yeah, I know, we're not using the 'journey' metaphor, but you get the idea. It's about growing, learning, and stepping up, bit by bit. So grab those opportunities, learn from the leaders you admire, and don't be afraid to be the newbie. Every experience is a stepping stone to becoming a confident leader who makes things happen.

And who knows? The skills you build now could open doors you've never even imagined, from college opportunities to future careers. All it takes is that first step, that decision to try. So, why not? Dive into leadership, test the waters, and start making your mark. After all, the world needs good leaders, and one of them might just be you.

8.4 MAINTAINING FRIENDSHIPS THROUGH TRANSITIONS

Navigating the shift from middle school to high school is like upgrading to the latest version of your favorite video game—exciting, sure, but also packed with new levels that require some serious navigating skills, especially when it comes to friendships. It's like one day you're all in the same small boat, paddling together, and the next, everyone's launched into different oceans, trying to find where they fit in the vast waters of high school life. This transition can stretch friendships as different schools, evolving interests, and new social groups introduce waves that might rock your social boat.

Let's talk strategies for keeping your middle school friendships afloat and thriving. Regular meet-ups are key. They're the lifebuoys that keep you connected in the swirling sea of new high school experiences. Plan monthly pizza nights or movie marathons. It doesn't have to be fancy—just something that keeps the connection lively. What about those friends who now live too far for regular hangouts? Technology to the rescue! Set up online gaming sessions where you can battle zombies or build empires while chatting about everything from new school dramas to old inside jokes. Apps like Discord or Skype can make these sessions run smoother than a skateboard down a fresh ramp.

Shared activities are another great glue for old friendships. Maybe you all join a fantasy football league or start a book club. This keeps you sharing experiences and growing together, even when you're physically apart. It's like keeping your roots intertwined, no matter how far your branches stretch. And don't forget the power of spontaneous connections. A quick text or a funny meme can bridge the gap between meet-ups, keeping the friendship vibrant.

Now, while you're steering the ship of old friendships, there's also the exciting task of charting courses to new ones. High school is a treasure trove of new faces and potential friends. The key here is openness. Join clubs, try out for sports teams, or volunteer in new activities—each one is a portal to new friendships. It's like each club or team is a different puzzle piece, and the more you collect, the clearer the picture of your high school social life becomes.

Building these new friendships means showing genuine interest in others. Ask questions, listen (really listen) to what your peers are saying, and offer your own stories and insights. It's like planting seeds—you must water them with attention and care to grow into strong connections. Remember, every senior you look up to in awe was once a newbie, too. Most are usually eager to include freshmen in activities, so don't be shy to jump into discussions or ask about the ropes of high school life.

Balancing old and new friendships is a bit like juggling. It requires awareness and practice not to drop the balls. Make sure you're not so wrapped up in new high school adventures that you drift away from old friends who've been with you through thick and thin. Conversely, don't cling so tightly to past friendships that you miss out on amazing new connections. It's all about finding that sweet spot where you can treasure the old while embracing the new.

So, as you navigate these exciting but sometimes choppy waters of friendship transitions, remember to anchor yourself in openness and effort. With some planning, a dash of courage, and a whole lot of heart, you'll find that maintaining old friendships while blossoming new ones isn't just possible; it's one of the most rewarding parts of moving through life's big changes. Keep paddling through both familiar and uncharted waters, and you'll build a fleet of friendships that can sail with you through anything high school throws your way.

8.5 PERSONAL SAFETY: TIPS FOR GROWING INDEPENDENCE

Ah, high school! It's like stepping onto a bigger stage. Bright lights, bigger roles, and, yes, more freedom. Suddenly, you're the one managing your after-school time, deciding whether to hit the books, join a club, or hang out with friends. This newfound independence is pretty awesome, but it's kind of like getting your first phone. It's super exciting, yet it comes with a few rules to keep things running smoothly.

Managing this freedom responsibly is key. Filling every spare minute with activities and social events is tempting, but balancing this with your schoolwork and some downtime is crucial. Think of your time as a giant pizza. You wouldn't eat it all in one go, right? So, why try to cram every activity into one day? Plan your week like you'd slice that pizza. Some slices go to schoolwork, some to clubs or sports, and others to chilling out. This way, everything gets its share without overwhelming you. And hey, if you need to shuffle things around a bit, that's cool. Flexibility is your friend when you're learning to juggle your new responsibilities.

Now, let's talk about staying safe when you're exploring new territories, like attending events or checking out different parts of town. High school might bring opportunities to attend concerts, sports events, or parties. Exciting? Absolutely! However, stepping into unfamiliar situations requires a bit of savvy. Always keep your crew in the loop about where you're going. Use the buddy system because, like in any good adventure movie, there's safety in numbers. And always have a plan for getting home—know your bus routes, have a rideshare app ready, or arrange a pick-up with someone you trust. It's like going on a treasure hunt; preparing your map and tools beforehand is crucial for a successful quest.

Speaking of safety, let's not forget the digital realms—social media and online interactions. High school usually means more social media buzz, which can be fun but also a bit of a minefield. Tweaking your privacy settings on social platforms can be as important as locking your front door. Make sure you're sharing content only with people you trust, not the whole world. Be mindful about what you post. Ask yourself, "Would I be cool with my grandma or my future employer seeing this?" If the answer's no, maybe keep it off the internet. And online harassment? Shut it down fast. Report it, block the person, and talk to an adult if things get creepy. Keeping your online life-friendly and clean is like keeping your room tidy; it makes it a more pleasant place to hang out.

Lastly, let's touch on a serious skill—self-defense. Now, I'm not talking about turning you into a ninja, but knowing a few basic moves can be empowering. It's not just about protecting yourself; it's about feeling confident in your ability to do so. Consider taking a basic self-defense class; sometimes, schools or community centers offer them. These classes teach you more than just moves —they boost your awareness of your surroundings, helping you spot and avoid sketchy situations before they escalate. Think of it as adding a security alarm to your personal space.

Navigating the bigger world of high school safely and responsibly isn't just about following rules; it's about using your freedom wisely. It's about making smart choices, whether you're planning your week, hanging out in new places, managing your digital footprint, or learning how to defend yourself. With each wise choice, you're not just keeping yourself safe; you're building a foundation of responsibility and confidence that'll serve you way beyond high school. So, embrace your new independence, but remember, with great power comes great responsibility. And you, my friend, are more than up to the challenge.

8.6 REFLECTING ON MIDDLE SCHOOL: LESSONS LEARNED AND LOOKING AHEAD

Ah, middle school! It's been a wild ride, hasn't it? From those first-day jitters to finally figuring out the best table in the cafeteria, you've grown so much. But as you stand on the brink of high school, it's the perfect time to grab a metaphorical mirror and take a good look at what you've learned about yourself during these transformative years. Self-reflection isn't just about patting yourself on the back or giving yourself a tough talk; it's about understanding your growth and setting the stage for future success.

Think about the academic hills you've climbed. Maybe algebra was a beast until you finally tamed it, or perhaps a history project sparked a love for storytelling. Each subject wasn't just about getting grades but about discovering what makes your brain buzz. And it's not just book smarts—those group projects taught you about teamwork and that science fair mishap? A lesson in bouncing back from setbacks. Reflecting on these experiences helps you pinpoint not just what you're good at but what you enjoy. It's like gathering clues on a treasure map, where X marks your potential future successes.

Now, let's talk about the challenges and victories. Remember that time you tried out for the school play and won a speaking part? That victory wasn't just about getting the part; it was about realizing you could. Or think about the times you felt overwhelmed by everything piling up but somehow managed to get through it all. These moments are gold mines for lessons on resilience and managing pressure—skills that are golddust in high school.

Setting goals based on these reflections can be super empowering as you gear up for the next big stage. It's not just about deciding whether to nail your grades or make new friends; it's about setting intentions that align with your discovered interests and strengths. It could be aiming to join the debate team because you've realized you've got a knack for arguing your point, or it's about taking advanced art classes because that project on mural design lit up something inside you.

And hey, while you're at it, why not celebrate all that growth? You've navigated the choppy waters of middle school, from acing tests and making friends to handling the tough days. Each step has been a building block in the awesome person you're becoming. So, give yourself a high-five, do a little happy dance in your room, or just take a moment to smile about it all. Celebrating isn't just about feeling good; it's a way to reinforce your positive strides, anchoring them as stepping stones for what's next.

As this chapter of your life closes and you gear up for the high school journey, carry forward the memories, lessons, and insights you've gathered. They're your armor and tools for the adventures ahead. Middle school might be ending, but your story—oh, it's just getting started.

So, keep that head high, your reflections close, and your goals set. High school is ready for you; with all you've learned and planned, you're more than prepared for it.

As we wrap up this reflection on your middle school years, remember that these lessons form the foundation of the exciting chapters ahead. You're stepping into high school with a toolkit brimming with knowledge, self-awareness, and aspirations. Let's carry this momentum forward, using our past to propel us into future triumphs. Up next, we dive into the practical world of managing your time effectively in high school—a critical skill for making the most of the coming years. Stay tuned; the best is yet to come!

CONCLUSION

Wow, what a ride it's been, right? From the first jitters of stepping into middle school to now, where you're gearing up to dive into the big leagues of high school and beyond. You've navigated through the choppy waters of social dynamics, learned to ride the roller coaster of emotions, tackled the wild jungle of academics, and even balanced the tightrope of online and offline worlds. Not to mention, you've explored the vast landscapes of extracurricular activities and started sketching out the paths to your future.

Let's do a quick flashback, shall we? We started with mastering the art of friendship and real-life connections in a world that sometimes feels like it exists more online than off. You've learned how to spot a true friend, handle the peer pressure like a pro, and steer clear of the drama that can make school feel like a soap opera. And remember all those tips about being kind online and keeping your digital footprint as neat as your room (or maybe neater)?

We then dove deep into understanding your emotions and those of others, turning you into an empathy ninja. Those skills are your secret weapons for building strong relationships and acing group projects. And let's not forget all the strategies we covered for acing your studies without burning out—because, let's face it, you've got enough on your plate without adding stress to the menu.

You've also discovered the joy of extracurriculars, from sports that pump up your energy levels to arts that feed your soul and volunteering that expands your heart. Each of these activities wasn't just fun—they were building blocks for the awesome person you're becoming.

We shared stories, too—real tales of triumph and hiccups from other middle schoolers just like you. Remember Emily's comeback in math or Lucas navigating the tricky social waters with courage? Each story was a reminder that you're not alone in this journey.

And resilience—boy, did we pump that muscle! You've learned that setbacks aren't stop signs; they're just signs that say, "Hey, there's another way to try this." You have the tools to bounce back from anything stronger and wiser.

Now, as you stand on the threshold of your next big adventure, remember that middle school was never just about getting through. It was about discovering who you are and want to become. The challenges, the wins, the oops moments—they were all part of this incredible journey of self-discovery. They were stepping stones, not stumbling blocks.

So, what's next? Start putting these strategies into action. Don't wait for the "perfect" moment—it doesn't exist. What does exist is today, right now, and it's the best time to start shaping your future. Set small goals, lean on your squad, and keep that chin up, even on the tough days. And remember, you've got a whole team in your corner—parents, teachers, friends, and yes, even me, through these pages, cheering you on.

Keep exploring, keep learning, and stay open to all the amazing possibilities your future holds. The world is vast, and your potential is limitless. So take a deep breath, pack your backpack with optimism and courage, and step into high school with a smile. You're ready for this. You're built for this. And I can't wait to see all the incredible places you'll go.

Here's to you and your future, and I hope you make the high school years genuinely spectacular. You've got this, and don't you forget it!

You've made it through the guide, and now you're ready to tackle middle school like a pro! With everything you've learned, you're set to face any challenge that comes your way. But there's one more thing you can do: share your knowledge with others.

By leaving your honest review on Amazon, you'll help other middle schoolers, parents, teachers, and even grandparents find the same support and confidence you now have. Your review could be the reason someone else finds the courage to navigate middle school with success!

Thank you so much for helping me keep the middle school survival guide alive. By sharing your experience, you're passing on the tools and tips that can make someone else's middle school journey just a little bit easier.

Scan the QR code to leave your review on Amazon:

Thank you for being part of this! Your review makes a real impact.

I appreciate your help more than you know!

DebbieAnn Lewis

ANSWER KEYS

FRIENDSHIP SCENARIOS QUIZ

a) If you picked mostly A's

You're a great friend! You care about others and always try to help.

b) If you picked mostly B's

You could work on being more thoughtful towards your friends.

c) If you picked mostly C's

You might need to think more about how your actions affect others

DIGITAL PRIVACY CHECK-UP QUIZ

Mostly A's: *Caution Needed!*

You might be a bit too relaxed about your digital privacy. It's time to start thinking more carefully about how you protect your information online.

Mostly B's: *Getting There!*

You're aware of some privacy practices, but there's room for improvement. Keep learning and applying good habits to stay safe online.

Mostly C's: *Good Start!*

You're doing a pretty good job of protecting your privacy, but there's still more you can do to be even safer.

Mostly D's: *Privacy Pro!*

You're on top of your digital privacy! Keep up the great work, and continue being mindful of your online safety.

WHAT'S YOUR INNER SUPERHERO? QUIZ

Mostly A's – Speedster Hero!

You're full of energy and love action! Just like a speedster superhero, you're quick on your feet and always ready for the next challenge.

Mostly B's – Brainy Hero!

You have a sharp mind and love learning new things. Like a superhero with super intelligence, you solve problems with your smarts and love figuring things out.

Mostly C's – Sky Hero!

You're adventurous and love exploring new places. Like a hero who can fly, you're always looking for the next big adventure and enjoy freedom and excitement.

Mostly D's – Caring Hero!

You have a big heart and love helping others. Just like a hero with healing powers, you're always there to lend a hand and make sure everyone is feeling their best.

Use your answers to match the extracurricular activities that align best with your interests and skills!

Mostly A's: Expressive and Communicative

Ideal clubs or activities:

- School Newspaper
- Writing Club
- Debate Team
- Drama Club

Mostly B's: Creative and Imaginative

Ideal clubs or activities:

- Art Club
- Music Club
- Photography Club
- Drama/Theater Club

Mostly C's: Logical and Analytical

Ideal clubs or activities:

- Robotics Club
- Science Club
- Chess Club
- Mathletes

Mostly D's: Energetic and Competitive

Ideal clubs or activities:

- Sports Teams (e.g., basketball, soccer, track and field)
- Outdoor Adventure Club
- Dance Team
- Cheerleading Squad

Mostly E's: Responsible and Organized

Ideal clubs or activities:

- Student Council
- Community Service Club
- Event Planning Committee
- Peer Mentoring Program

REFERENCES

American Psychological Association. (n.d.). *Resilience for teens: 10 tips to build skills on bouncing back*. https://www.apa.org/topics/resilience/bounce-teens

New York University. (2015, October). *Middle schoolers may benefit academically from extracurricular activities*. https://www.nyu.edu/about/news-publications/news/2015/october/middle-schoolers-may-benefit-academically-from-extracurricular-activities.html

Mind24-7. (n.d.). *Teens, technology and friendships: Navigating the digital landscape*. https://www.mind24-7.com/blog/teens-technology-and-friendships-navigating-the-digital-landscape/

Brookes Publishing. (n.d.). *8 activities to boost students' emotional intelligence*. https://blog.brookespublishing.com/8-activities-to-boost-students-emotional-intelligence/

Youth.gov. (n.d.). *Involving youth in positive youth development*. https://youth.gov/youth-topics/involving-youth-positive-youth-development

KidsHealth. (n.d.). *How can I improve my self-esteem? (for teens)*. https://kidshealth.org/en/teens/self-esteem.html

American Academy of Child and Adolescent Psychiatry. (n.d.). *Stress management and teens*. https://www.aacap.org/AACAP/Families_and_Youth/Facts_for_Families/FFF-Guide/Helping-Teenagers-With-Stress-066.aspx

Care.com. (n.d.). *10 expert-backed time management tips for middle school students*. https://www.care.com/c/time-management-tips-for-middle-school-students/

KQED MindShift. (n.d.). *13 effective study strategies to help students learn*. https://www.kqed.org/mindshift/57644/13-effective-study-strategies-to-help-students-learn

Honor Society. (n.d.). *The impact of extracurricular activities on academic success*. https://www.honorsociety.org/articles/impact-extracurricular-activities-academic-success

Nemours KidsHealth. (n.d.). *Test anxiety (for teens)*. https://kidshealth.org/en/teens/test-anxiety.html#:

National Institutes of Health. (2022). *Social media–driven routes to positive mental health*. https://www.ncbi.nlm.nih.gov/pmc/articles/PMC8933808/

Common Sense Education. (n.d.). *Teachers' essential guide to cyberbullying

prevention*. https://www.commonsense.org/education/articles/teachers-essen
tial-guide-to-cyberbullying-prevention

TeachThought. (n.d.). *12 tips for students to manage their digital footprints*.
https://www.teachthought.com/the-future-of-learning/digital-footprints/

Raising Children Network. (n.d.). *Teenage screen time: Tips for balance*. https://
raisingchildren.net.au/teens/entertainment-technology/screen-time-healthy-
screen-use/healthy-screen-time-teens

Crimson Education. (n.d.). *Top 10 benefits of extracurricular activities in high
school*. https://www.crimsoneducation.org/us/blog/benefits-of-extracurricu
lar-activities/

SISU Guard. (n.d.). *How to balance school and sports: 9 tips for student athletes*.
https://blog.sisuguard.com/how-to-find-a-balance-between-school-and-sports

University of Chicago Consortium on School Research. (2019, June). *Arts education and social-emotional learning*. https://consortium.uchicago.edu/sites/
default/files/2019-05/Arts%20Education%20and%20Social-Emotional-
June2019-Consortium%20and%20Ingenuity.pdf

DoSomething.org. (n.d.). *The ultimate guide to volunteering for teens*. https://
dosomething.org/article/the-ultimate-guide-to-volunteering-for-teens

Family Education. (n.d.). *5 sensational school success stories*. https://www.fami
lyeducation.com/school-learning/your-childs-school/5-sensational-school-
success-stories

HelpGuide.org. (n.d.). *Deal with a bully and overcome bullying*. https://www.
helpguide.org/articles/abuse/bullying.htm

ERIC. (2019). *The benefits of participating in extracurricular activities*. https://
files.eric.ed.gov/fulltext/EJ1230758.pdf

High Speed Training. (n.d.). *Communication in the classroom: Skills for teachers*.
https://www.highspeedtraining.co.uk/hub/communication-skills-for-teachers/

Newport Academy. (n.d.). *Building resilience in children and teens*. https://www.
newportacademy.com/resources/well-being/resilience-in-teens/

PositivePsychology.com. (n.d.). *Positive education: Applying positive psychology
in schools*. https://positivepsychology.com/positive-education-happy-
students/

Harvard Summer School. (n.d.). *Why celebrating small wins matters*. https://
summer.harvard.edu/blog/why-celebrating-small-wins-matters/

Medical News Today. (n.d.). *18 mindfulness activities for teens and students*.
https://www.medicalnewstoday.com/articles/mindfulness-activities-for-teens

Summit Learning Charter. (n.d.). *10 ways to easily transition from middle school
to high school*. https://summitlearningcharter.org/about-us/blog/middle-
school-to-high-school-transition/

Ohio Department of Education. (n.d.). *Middle school (6-8) activities*. http://

education.ohio.gov/Topics/Career-Tech/Career-Connections/In-Demand-Jobs-Week-Toolkit/Middle-School-6-8-Activities

The YES Canada. (n.d.). *Developing leadership for teens*. https://www.theyes.ca/post/developing-teen-leadership

National Library of Medicine. (2022). *The academic benefits of maintaining friendships across demographic divides*. https://pubmed.ncbi.nlm.nih.gov/35618366/